ALL THE RAGE

A HISTORY OF FASHION AND TRENDS

ALL THE RAGE
A HISTORY OF FASHION AND TRENDS

BY THE EDITORS OF TIME-LIFE BOOKS

TIME®
LIFE

CONTENTS

1
THE BODY BEAUTIFUL

Making the most of it: Surgery and silicone . . . waist watchers . . . mighty Atlas . . . effortless exercise . . . run for your life . . . giant killers . . . judicious jaw-boning . . . injectable youth

2
IMPROVING ON NATURE

Best face forward: Ancient unguents . . . packs Romana . . . patches of prettiness . . . pale poison . . . film Factor . . . big hair . . . ruling the waves . . . charm school . . . body art . . . nailing it down . . . pleasing perforations

3
THE GLASS OF FASHION

Style follows strength: Tunics and tights . . . ruffing it . . . British black . . . power suits . . . Redcoats to khakis . . . late bloomers . . . Atalanta's race . . . mountain of youth . . . killer shoes

4
TRENDSETTERS

Movers, shakers, and sharp dressers: Royal stylists . . . a taste of Brummell . . . Chanel number one . . . gentleman golfer . . . Charles Dana Gibson's girl . . . film visions . . . Twiggy . . . out of Egypt . . . Xow of shows

THE BODY BEAUTIFUL

Men and women have been drawn by the flame of vanity since the dawn of human memory, searching, often futilely, for ideal physical beauty. Their failure to find it does not mean that the body beautiful is unattainable, however—only that the chimera of beauty does not keep the same form for very long. Following the will-o'-the-wisp of anatomical fashion, muscles must alternately expand grotesquely or nearly disappear, stomachs flatten or distend, complexions flicker between dark and pale. Skin must be abraded, cheekbones raised, faces lifted, breasts augmented, and waists constrained, all in the name of perceived beauty.

Once there were limits—no matter how one longed for change, at some point physique and heredity provided barriers to further alteration. Now human ingenuity has found ways to produce even the most implausible anatomical realignments, eschewing exercise and diet, the real tools of body shaping, for an array of radical techniques: binding, cutting, stitching, squeezing, drugging, implanting, and eroding until the desired contours are achieved. Expensive, often surpassingly painful, sometimes cruel, attempts to wrench the body into a new configuration can also be dangerous. Among the beauty seekers, many are badly scorched—many perish—when they flutter too near the terrible flame, trading their lives for ephemeral, and illusory, perfection.

Heady Distinction

Ever since the founding of Jericho some 10,000 years ago—and perhaps long before—some parents have squeezed, stretched, kneaded, and bound the soft bones of their infant children's skulls, flattening or elongating them in the interest of fashion. The ancient Egyptians admired elongated heads and wrapped strips of cotton cloth around their babies' skulls for the first year, to encourage growth of the same elongated shape sported by Queen Nefertiti and other members of the royal family. Head-binding was also common in Europe—especially France and Holland—until the 18th century. The practice persists among the Mangbetu women of the Sudan, who deform their infants' heads by wrapping them with thin strips of hemp or cotton.

The Indian tribes of America's Pacific Northwest used various bindings and boards to shape their skulls, tribal fashion dictating whether the desired shape would be cylindrical or sloping in front or back to denote beauty and social status. The Chinooks of the Pacific Northwest squeezed their children's foreheads between two boards, simultaneously flattening the back of the skull and creating a very low forehead that sloped up to an exaggerated peak in the back. The sharper the angle, the more distinguished the person.

Not all shaped skulls were intended; the Chippewa of North America bound their children to cradleboards so they would grow straight and vigorous and be easier to tend. As a side effect, the boards flattened the children's heads. And a tribe whose members did not mold their children's crania were known by the distinctive shape of their skulls: the Flatheads of western Montana. □

Losing Face

For years, the Chinese slang terms for Westerners—Big Noses and Round Eyes—clearly demonstrated the contempt with which most Asians viewed European notions of beauty. But not all Orientals shun the West. "Many young people have very Western minds, and think that the Western look is very beautiful," explains one Shanghai beautician. "So a lot of young men and women perm their hair and do other things to look more Western."

For those who want a more permanent transformation than an altered hair style, however, surgery is the thing. The most popular operation is blepharoplasty, in which a small amount of skin and fat is removed from the upper eyelid, making the eye appear larger and rounder and creating the crease typical of Caucasian eyelids. The procedure can be done to both eyes in as little as 20 minutes. The second most common operation is rhinoplasty, in which a silicone strip is inserted into the nose, raising and enlarging it. Even in the People's Republic of China, where Western styles are frequently censured, occidental faces have become popular—every day in Shanghai about 100 women undergo eye lifts, and about half that number have their noses enlarged.

The surgery originated in Japan after World War II and quickly spread throughout East Asia. Today in Hong Kong, Taiwan, and the Philippines, eyelid surgery is done by beauticians who charge about $500. In the United States, most medical insurance policies do not cover cosmetic surgery, and physicians charge far more—between $900 and $4,000—for the same operation. The price disparity has led some Asian-Americans to have themselves inexpensively western-ized when they visit the Far East to renew old family ties.

Often, however, cheap surgery is just that. One Los Angeles doctor reports that one-fifth of his Asian blepharoplasty patients are seeking surgery to correct problems with their cut-rate incisions. Medical considerations aside, the practice offends those who ask why Asians should wish to conform to a Western ideal of beauty, rather than embracing Asia's own formidable aesthetic. "Cutting eyes is like footbinding," says the Chinese-American writer Maxine Hong Kingston, referring to a 1,000-year-old Chinese practice that was eradicated earlier in the century *(pages 32-33)*. "It's not creative. It's a mutilation and a perversion." □

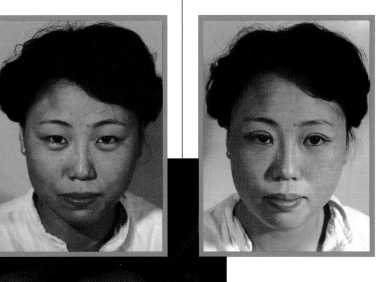

An Asian woman's eyelids *(above, left)* show folds of skin that were later removed by blepharoplasty for a more Western look *(above)*. Preparing for a similar operation, the Chinese patient at left shuts her eyes so that the lids can be marked with dotted lines to guide the surgeon.

Hollow Cheeks

In 1978 Elaine Young was a slim, blonde, attractive, well-connected, and successful Beverly Hills realtor. The daughter of a movie studio executive and once married to actor Gig Young, Elaine was a friend to many Hollywood stars. But she was also 42 years old that year and troubled that her own appearance was not measuring up to the movieland ideal.

Young's vague unease about her looks was focused one day when a friend walked into her office sporting, as she put it later, "cheekbones even Katharine Hepburn might envy." The chiseled cheeks were not a gift of nature but the product of multiple injections of liquid silicone, a 20th-century miracle chemical first used for industrial seals and lubricants. During the 1950s and 1960s, silicone, which is compatible with human tissue, was taken up by plastic and reconstructive surgeons to rebuild damaged tissue and bone—or to supply it where none had existed before. Dazzled by her visitor's evident success, Young decided on the spot that she, too, would have perfect cheekbones and called her friend's doctor for an appointment.

Before long Young's face looked as if it had been carved by the gods; she was delighted. Every few weeks, especially if she had a party or other special occasion coming up, she had her doctor add a little more lift with an injection. "Those 'little' silicone injections turned out to be a time bomb," she says. By mid-1979—about six months after she received her first injection—her face looked more inflamed than sculptured. She continued the injections until she again encountered her friend.

To Young's horror, the other woman's perfect cheekbones had deformed into a swollen, puffy mess. Young immediately stopped the course of injections, but it was already too late; by the end of 1980, her face was a bloated, bloodshot mass that had turned as hard as wood. Bit by bit, the silicone had shifted beneath her skin, wrapping around nerves, hardening, and forming scar tissue. When she sought help, her plastic surgeon would not return her telephone calls; other physicians said there was nothing they could do.

That was not quite true—there was a painful and uncertain alternative. For six years, Young underwent grueling injections of cortisone in an attempt to reduce the pain and swelling. In January 1987 a lump of silicone threatened to injure her vision, and surgery was needed to remove it. More surgery followed. Time and again doctors operated to remove hardened lumps of silicone that pressed on nerves and tried to erupt from beneath Young's skin. By 1992 she had undergone 32 operations. Yet more silicone remained, pain and swelling persisted, and more surgery lay in the future. Nevertheless, Young's face—once attractive, then ruined by injection—was returning to its original condition. It had taken more than a dozen years of agony for her to come full circle, she sums up bitterly, "all because I wanted to be pretty." □

Her face still badly swollen from silicone injections in this 1989 photograph, fashionable Beverly Hills realtor Elaine Young is seen with her new Jaguar convertible in the Hollywood Hills.

Pumping Plastic

Surgical beautification, once almost the exclusive domain of women, is winning new converts among men. A decade ago, males accounted for only about 1 cosmetic surgery patient in 10; today nearly a third of all such surgical procedures are performed on men, forcing doctors to pioneer new techniques tailored to the unique demands of male vanity.

Most men go under the knife for the same reasons that women do; they want straighter noses, thinner thighs, or a face less scoured by time. For a few, surgery is a route to economic survival: They hope looking younger will help them compete in a tough job market. Some men, too, are motivated by a desire to perfect physiques already molded by hours of exercise and weightlifting, but still somehow incomplete. "It was strictly vanity and ego that made me do it," says Gary Gordon, an amateur bodybuilder in Oklahoma City. "But if you want to look sexier, why not?" He received calf implants in 1985 to compensate for skinny legs that had defied every known calf exercise.

Males have also turned toward their equivalent of the female breast implant, but with a difference. Where women's implants are soft and pliant, implants for males are made of a solid silicone polymer that has been used for many years in rebuilding chest deformi-

Chest closeups of one of Mel Bircoll's male patients show how sagging pectoral muscles *(above)* firmed up *(left)* after the Beverly Hills, California, plastic surgeon inserted solid silicone strips through the armpit.

ties caused by birth defects or accidental injury. The implants, added beneath the patient's pectorals, are carefully molded to give the appearance of rock-hard, well-conditioned muscle. "We're looking for the hard body," explains Dr. Mel Bircoll, the Beverly Hills, California, plastic surgeon who created the procedure for pectoral implants. "We're not looking for a mushy soft body."

Hard bodies come at a price: Pectoral implants cost about $6,500, calves $5,000 per pair. The chest-swelling operation, which involves slipping several five-inch-long silicone slugs through an incision in the armpit, requires sev-

eral weeks of recuperation during which mobility is limited and the risk of infection or internal bleeding is always present. Less easy to assess are the long-term risks. Although the hard implants are not prone to the silicone leaks and deformations that may plague women's breast implants, some surgeons worry that men's silicone slabs could slip grotesquely out of place or erode the underlying bone. Others say it is too early to tell, although some modified males have reported severe rashes and itching. Still, most men in search of a bigger, prettier, harder body put such doubts behind them as they turn to such innovations as the latest made-to-order muscle: the buttock implant. □

Beauty Queen

Elizabeth Wittelsbach was one of the loveliest young women Europe had ever seen, and her charms won her an emperor's heart. But behind the facade of regal beauty, she was ruled by a most unimperial obsession with form and physical fitness that isolated her from reality, distanced her from her family and subjects, and left her bitter and alone at the end of her life.

Nicknamed Sisi, Elizabeth was the second daughter of the gently eccentric Duke Maximilian of Bavaria—better known as Duke Max. His idea of entertainment was to dress up as an itinerant musician and play at fairs for the coins thrown by village yokels. He also loved horses and introduced Elizabeth to riding when she was very young. She showed such natural aptitude that the duke once told her, "If you and I, Sisi, had not been born princes, we would have been performers in a circus."

But Elizabeth was destined for greater things. In August of 1853 she accompanied her mother and older sister Helene to Austria, where Helene was to become the bride of the young emperor Francis Joseph. The wedding plans changed, however, when the 23-

year-old monarch set eyes on Sisi, then a tall, slender 15-year-old whose head was wreathed in shining auburn braids. The emperor was enchanted. Sisi's response was mixed. "Of course I love him," the young girl said when she heard that the emperor wished to marry her. "How could I help but love him. If only he were not an Emperor." Then she burst into tears. Within a year, the imperial pair had married. Just two weeks after the wedding, a somewhat disillusioned Elizabeth wrote: "Oh had I but never left the path / That would have led me to freedom. / Oh that on the broad avenues / Of vanity I had never strayed!"

Having strayed, however, Elizabeth embraced her duties with a vengeance. Although she had once confessed to a favored niece that she "loathed the whole business of child-bearing," she bore four children. Embarrassed by the physical changes of pregnancy, she concealed her swollen body from public view while carrying her first child, the archduchess Sophia, in 1855. To the horror of her mother-in-law, the old archduchess Sophia, Elizabeth was riding barely a month after the baby's birth. As the children were quickly whisked off to their grandmother's side, Elizabeth found herself increasingly isolated from them—and not inclined by temperament to show them much affection when she had the opportunity. Eventually, she was spending more time each day having her waist-length hair brushed and dressed than she spent with her children. The empress had escaped into vanity.

Always proud of her slim figure—she stood five and a half feet tall and rarely weighed more than 110 pounds—Elizabeth sustained her slender form with obsessive dieting and exercise, including riding, marathon walking, fencing, and gymnastics—she even had a small gymnasium set up in her room in the Schönbrunn Palace. She weighed herself twice a day, and if she exceeded 110 pounds by even an ounce, she immediately imposed a diet of oranges and raw meat juice. Needless to say, her odd habits were noticed and much gossiped about; the prince of Hesse called her "almost inhumanly slender." Elizabeth emphasized her slenderness by binding herself tightly in satin and moiré corsets ordered from Paris; the lacing up sometimes took an hour.

Despite the draconian diets, or perhaps because of them, Elizabeth remained a tremendous athlete, lauded as one of the best riders in Europe, equally skilled at hunting, circus trick riding, and dressage. During one visit to England, a tailor was summoned each morning to sew her riding skirt onto her bodice, so that not a wrinkle would mar the splendor of her waist, which measured just 18 inches even after she had borne four children. Said one British aristocrat approvingly, the 44-year-old empress "looked like an angel and rode like the devil."

The empress remained fond of her husband, but once the first flush of love faded the pair had found little in common—he sober, patient, delighting in the comforts of home and family, she high-strung, self-absorbed, uninterested in politics, and plagued by depression and hypochondria. Her trips abroad became more frequent—as Romanian queen Carmen Sylva put it, "She has hidden wings, which she spreads, and flies away whenever she finds the world unbearable." Perhaps to compensate for her estrangement from her family, Elizabeth actively abetted Francis Joseph's longstanding chaste friendship with Katharina Schratt, a popular actress.

Walpurga Paget, the German-born wife of Britain's ambassador to Vienna, described 45-year-old Elizabeth at a court ball. "She does not look a day over 32," wrote Lady Paget. "She is very tall but does not appear so because of her excessive slightness. Not only is her waist slim, but she is narrow across the chest and shoulders and accentuates the smallness of her hips by the way her dresses are made, quite clinging and without a single pleat round the waist, contrary to present fashion." Elizabeth's eyes were brown, "with a pretty childlike expression, though something irresponsible lurks in them. Her lips, bright red, are always closed in a quiet smile, because, like all her family, she has discoloured teeth. Her complexion is rather weatherbeaten from excessive riding and walking, but she has a pretty pink colour in her cheeks." She wore a flowered white damask dress, and "round her throat, over her bodice and round the waist were rivers of emeralds and diamonds." Although still a striking woman, Elizabeth was no longer Europe's reigning beauty.

But more than Elizabeth's beauty was in decline. Her empire trembled, as Europe slid toward anarchy, war, and revolution, and her life sank into melancholy. In 1889 Elizabeth was devastated by the death of her only son, 31-year-old crown prince Rudolf, in a sordid murder-suicide pact with the ◊

18-year-old baroness Marie Vetsera at Mayerling, the family hunting lodge near Vienna. A year later Elizabeth's dearest friend passed away, another in a general dying off of those she loved. Now the empress's rides, daylong hikes, and lengthy travels became more and more compulsive and less pleasurable. "Everything had to be done to excess, if only to escape from herself," commented Carmen Sylva. "They have tried to harness this fairy being to rigid etiquette and empty forms, but the fairy being cannot endure bolts or bars, or any form of servitude or restraint."

In fact, the fairy being was no longer much in evidence. After Crown Prince Rudolf's suicide, Elizabeth dressed herself in deep and permanent mourning, and the depressions and skin rashes that had troubled her adult life intensified. By 1898, her fine face ravaged by a kind of eczema, Elizabeth had begun keeping to the shadows, a lonely wraith in crepe, living at a clinic in Switzerland.

On September 9, invited for a rare outing to the baroness Rothschild's estate at Pregny across Lake Geneva, the 61-year-old empress ignored warnings of political unrest and spent the day there. But as she stepped aboard the lake steamer that would take her home, an Italian anarchist attacked her with a sharpened file. Elizabeth fell, then seemed to recover, and shakily boarded the boat. Moments later, she fainted. Only then did her attendant notice a tiny, crusted perforation in her breast—a wound that had fatally penetrated her heart, but scarcely bled outside the tourniquet of her tightly laced bodice. Moments later, Elizabeth of Austria was dead. □

Strait-Laced

It was no simple matter to be New York City's most talked-about woman at the turn of the 20th century, but entertainer Anna Held managed—and then some. Held was a chanteuse, a singer of seductive and saucy songs. But her most famous attribute was her slight frame, pinched in the middle by an 18-inch waist—the quintessential hourglass figure of her day.

Anna Held was an exotic import, born in Poland but claiming Paris as her home, where she established her musical reputation. She traveled to the United States by way of London, where she was discovered during a singing engagement by the 25-year-old American impresario Florenz Ziegfeld. Although Ziegfeld's intentions at the time were more commercial than romantic, he wooed Held as if he were an ardent suitor, sending a basket of rare orchids and a diamond bracelet to her dressing room. These and other blandishments so impressed Held that she gave up her European career, left her infant daughter and South American husband, and headed for New York, where Ziegfeld made her the star of a popular farce.

Held arrived in New York with a splash—into a milk-filled bathtub, surrounded by a room full of wide-eyed reporters—and her sensational reputation was instantly established. Soon American audiences were mad for the pert gamine who cooed such coy lyrics as, "Won't you come and play wiz me?"

Even Ziegfeld was entranced, and his commercial interest soon became personal. Held divorced her husband and married her impresario. The pair reigned as the royal couple of show business for the first decade of the century. She set a standard of feminine beauty, while he manipulated the media to hold the attention of her fans with publicity accounts, for example, of her having single-handedly halted a runaway horse. To the public, Held was a hot-blooded, brave, and beautiful alternative to an imaginary, and less approachable, female paradigm of the day, the statuesque, athletic, independent Gibson Girl *(pages 117-118)*.

But, in her own way, Held was no more real than her aristocratic counterpart. The singer achieved her vaunted waspish waist through the use of painfully tight corsets and, it was rumored, surgical removal of her lowest ribs. Few, if any, members of the public were ready to emulate Held's slimming surgery, but they clamored to share her accessories. Held may have been the first celebrity to trade on her fame with marketing tie-ins; after her greatest stage triumph, *Ziegfeld's Follies* of 1907, Anna Held corsets, face powder, and pomade leaped off the shelves.

By its nature, however, celebrity lives on the whims of others. Although her beauty was esteemed by an adoring public, Held's career was the creation of her husband. After 1910 Florenz Ziegfeld found new women to woo and idols to promote. No longer in demand in New York and separated romantically and professionally from Ziegfeld, Held took to the road, performing on both sides of the Atlantic before World War I and starring in a 1915 film, *Madame la Présidente.* The end came in January 1918, soon after Held col-

lapsed in Milwaukee while touring with a musical, *Follow Me.* The doctor's initial diagnosis— "lacing too tight with corsets"—gave way to the far more serious findings of myeloma, a disorder of the spinal cord, and pernicious anemia. Anna Held died in August of that year, and the ideal she had represented quickly followed her to the grave. The hourglass figure was gone, replaced by the determinedly shapeless flappers of the Roaring Twenties. □

Jauntily dressed for one of her early stage roles —and to accentuate her remarkable hourglass figure—Anna Held smiles at the camera in an 1897 publicity shot taken shortly after her splashy arrival in the United States.

Copyright 1897. by W.M.Morrison.

Waists of Time

European knights returning from the Crusades of the 11th, 12th, and 13th centuries deluged their homelands with new wealth and fresh, foreign notions of beauty and style. The noblemen of Europe now expected women of their class to be sensuous, sensitive, and grateful for the protective strength of their men. The ladies agreed and the word *élégance* took its place in the French vocabulary, signifying refinement, grace, and beauty. The impact of such ideas was swift and enduring. European women revealed that there were contours beneath their formerly shapeless robes by adopting garments that followed and accentuated the lines of the female body. And the waistline—thicker, thinner, higher, lower—became the moving baseline of fashionable femininity.

The function of clothing also changed. No longer could a garment simply drape revealingly upon its wearer—now clothes actually forced their wearers' waistlines into the configuration of the day. For seven centuries since, women's clothes have bound, clamped, laced, and braced their bodies into the prevailing perfect figure. □

The high waistline and pregnant look that were popular in the 14th century caused these Italian noblewomen to waddle fashionably about with their stomachs protruding and their hips flared.

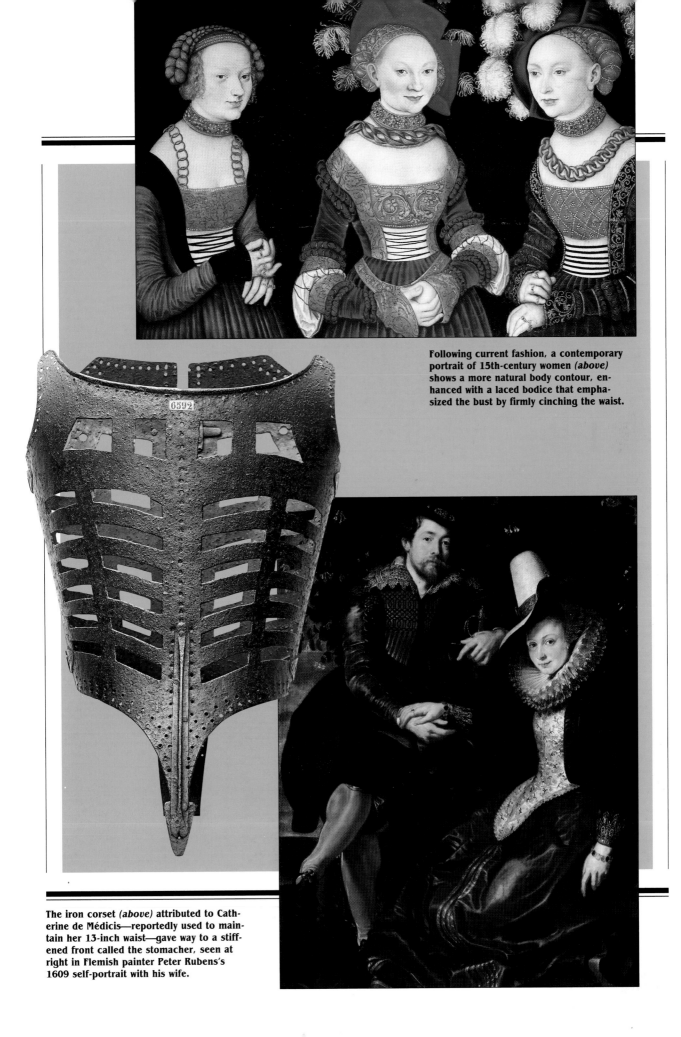

Following current fashion, a contemporary portrait of 15th-century women *(above)* shows a more natural body contour, enhanced with a laced bodice that emphasized the bust by firmly cinching the waist.

The iron corset *(above)* attributed to Catherine de Médicis—reportedly used to maintain her 13-inch waist—gave way to a stiffened front called the stomacher, seen at right in Flemish painter Peter Rubens's 1609 self-portrait with his wife.

The low, narrow waistlines of the 17th century were formed by conical bodices like the one pictured at right, covered in linen or damask and stiffened with stays made of wood or whalebone.

Glory Bound

During the late 16th century, the female form—following the lead of the women of Spain's mighty court—hid within sweeping skirts supported by huge constructions of felt, horsehair, and metal. But no matter how broad the dress, the medieval stricture of the waist persisted, tightly bound by an external corset appropriately called a stomacher. The result was a torso shaped like an inverted cone. For the next two centuries, the corset intensified its war on waists, adding rigid stays and heavy lacing to the squeezing apparatus—and the term *strait-laced* to the language.

Only in the late 18th century—the age of enlightenment and revolution—did the female waist find some relief. With the French Revolution, women, fearing to be seen as aristocratic, discarded the painful stays as a repugnant mark of gentility. When they next put on their corsets, some 20 years later, the device had become exclusively a piece of underwear, as it has remained. □

The woman in Dutch artist Jan Mytens's 1662 *Portrait of a Lady* is so tightly laced that her dress appears to be ribbed.

A 1778 French illustration *(left)* shows corsets becoming undergarments, laced in front for convenience and concealed by outer clothing. Constructed by specialty tailors, the garments were usually fitted with the husband present.

After the French Revolution, women dispensed with corsets as an artifact of aristocracy, favoring sheer "Empire" dresses like the one worn by Spain's Donna Joaquina Tellez-Giron in this 1798 portrait by the artist Augustin Esteve.

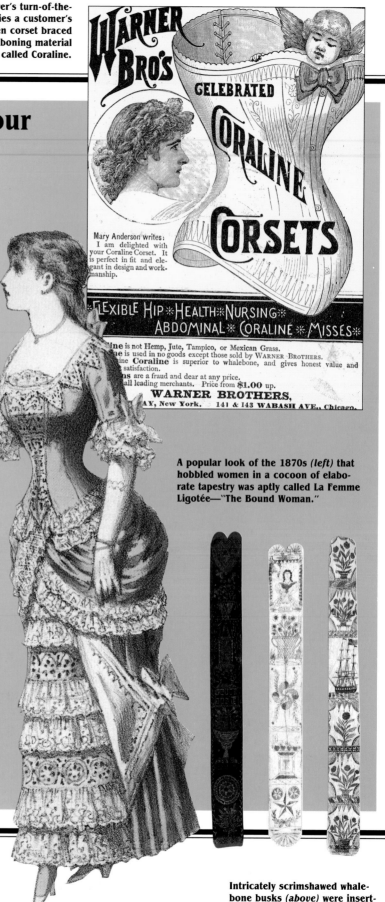

Shape of the Hour

The 19th-century romantic movement in music and literature was accompanied by a drop in the female waistline and a renewed pinching of the midriff, as in the past, with a tightly laced corset. Reinforced by artfully carved whalebone "busks," these devices encased their wearers' midriffs like rigid exoskeletons and squeezed the waist with unprecedented ferocity to create that paradigm of form the hourglass figure.

Bulging above and below a narrow waist, women of the period were so corseted that virtually every activity was impaired— breathing, eating, walking, and even standing. Doctors warned that pressure from corsets could damage and dislocate internal organs and ascribed a host of ailments and disabilities to them.

Perhaps sensing a groundswell of anticorset sentiment, manufacturers began advertising "healthy" corsets that purportedly did their work less painfully. The ads created such an appealing image of the apparatus that, as the 20th century opened, the corset was an established piece of female underclothing, without which few women felt fully dressed. □

A popular look of the 1870s *(left)* that hobbled women in a cocoon of elaborate tapestry was aptly called La Femme Ligotée—"The Bound Woman."

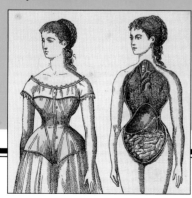

In this cautionary sketch, a too-tight corset overinflates a woman's lungs and causes the diaphragm to push her internal organs downward.

Intricately scrimshawed whalebone busks *(above)* were inserted into corsets in order to stiffen bustlines.

The secret scaffolding for the turn-of-the-century hourglass shape was an elongated corset *(right)* that laced up the back.

The epitome of tight lacing was reached in the sultry polonaise look—seen at left in British artist Charles Hermans's 1881 painting entitled *Circe*—in which undergarments built up the bust, cinched the waist, and padded the hips.

Like ambulatory hourglasses, models stroll beneath a fanciful arbor in this early-20th-century advertisement for the straight-front corset, designed to constrain their bodies to the S-shape then in vogue.

À LA SPIRITE

C/B

STRAIGHT FRONT CORSETS

For The ☐ of FASHI

Full Circle

Wasp-waisted British actress Camille Clifford *(left)* embodied the perfect form in the early 1900s. Beneath her gown a cruelly strait-laced corset held the fashionable form—and, to a degree, its wearer—breathlessly in place.

The coming of World War I, and the fact that more women sought physically active lives, destroyed the shapely paradigm. In the form that replaced it the waist was no longer cinched—giving ground to top-to-toe slimness. For the well endowed, however, flatness could not be attained without secret help from within. The full-bodied corset, reborn as a gartered girdle *(below),* renewed its grip on those who would be fashionably planar.

Then, in the 1950s, as Parisian haute couture revived after World War II, the hourglass figure was restored to favor and with it the bite of a constricting corset, albeit a modern, elasticized one. ☐

Modified with laces, buckles, and stocking garters, this predecessor of the modern girdle was popular with women during the First World War.

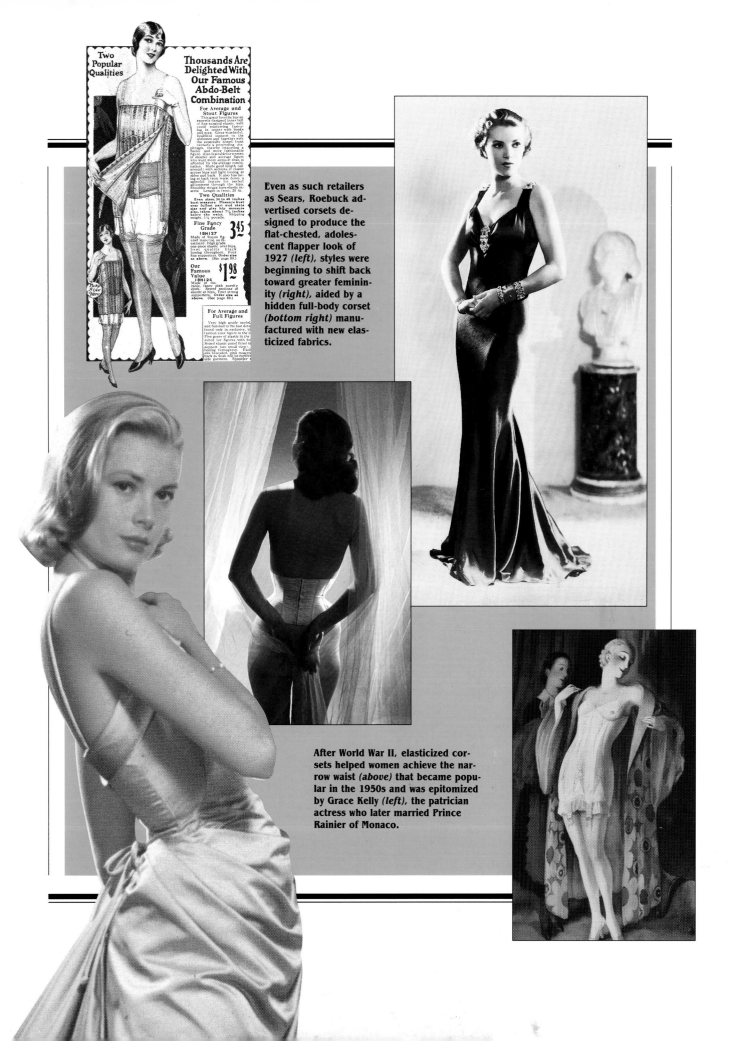

Even as such retailers as Sears, Roebuck advertised corsets designed to produce the flat-chested, adolescent flapper look of 1927 *(left)*, styles were beginning to shift back toward greater femininity *(right)*, aided by a hidden full-body corset *(bottom right)* manufactured with new elasticized fabrics.

After World War II, elasticized corsets helped women achieve the narrow waist *(above)* that became popular in the 1950s and was epitomized by Grace Kelly *(left)*, the patrician actress who later married Prince Rainier of Monaco.

Big Mac

In the early 1900s Angelo Siciliano was a scrawny immigrant lad so weakened by anemia that his parents moved to a ground-floor apartment in Brooklyn to spare him the effort of climbing stairs. Forbidden to take part in games and sports, the young Angelo took to visiting two of his borough's cultural oases, the Brooklyn Museum and the Prospect Park Zoo. Years later Siciliano recalled that on his visits to the museum he was captivated by the magnificent muscles depicted in the statue of the Greek hero Hercules. At the zoo, Siciliano wrote, he became entranced with muscle in motion, especially that of lions and tigers. He also took note of a paradox: The great cats spent hours lazing in their cages, yet they seemed to maintain their strength.

As he later told the story, Siciliano began to imitate the big cats, spending hours flexing and relaxing his muscles. By 1922 the once-sickly 29-year-old had found work as a vaudeville strongman and a model for heroic statuary. In front of the U.S. Treasury building in Washington, D.C., for example, a sculpted likeness of founding father Alexander Hamilton stands on a marble body modeled

by Angelo Siciliano. The young Brooklynite was so transformed by his exercise regimen that health guru Bernarr McFadden's *Physical Culture* magazine awarded him the title of "The World's Most Perfectly Developed Man."

His ambition fired by such attention, Siciliano changed his name to Charles Atlas, taking the surname from the Titan of Greek mythology who was condemned to bear the weight of the world on his shoulders. Armed with a new name that was a virtual synonym for strength, Atlas tried to cash in on his muscle-building techniques with mail-order marketing and sales through a New York gymnasium. The business languished until 1929, when Atlas encountered Charles Roman, a New York advertising executive who also happened to be an admirer.

Roman, who

claims to have obtained results from Atlas's exercises after only a week, set to work creating an advertisement that has since become a legendary artifact of American popular culture. Presented as a comic strip, it told the touching tale of a hollow-chested character named Mac, who has sand kicked in his face by a passing beach bully and is humiliated when he protests. Shunned as a weakling by his girl, the despondent Mac discovers Charles Atlas. A few weeks later, he is back on the beach, but now a muscleman himself; he dispatches the bully with a right jab and retrieves the admiration of his fickle girlfriend, who exclaims, "You ARE a real man after all!"

Mac's story of success was printed side by side with photographs of a tanned Charles Atlas clad in a leopard-skin brief. Those who responded to the ad could buy his 13-week bodybuilding course for a mere $30. For their money, buyers received a series of

First used in 1930, the classic Charles Atlas comic-strip advertisement changed little over the decades but kept up with the times. This 1960s version includes a reference to the muscleman's television commercials.

pamphlets that provided instruction in what Atlas called Dynamic Tension. The technique pits one muscle or group of muscles against another and—although Atlas also worked out with weights at the YMCA—requires no elaborate gym or heavy equipment.

Roman's appeals appeared in comic books, pulp magazines, newspapers, and on matchbook covers. Millions of young men apparently identified with Mac, for the orders poured in. By 1939 Charles Atlas had become a household name, and his depiction of himself as a one-time "97-pound weakling" entered the language.

Atlas's claims for Dynamic Tension were challenged by other mail-order strongmen, including the York, Pennsylvania, barbell manufacturer Robert C. Hoffman. "Dynamic hooey," huffed Hoffman, declaring that Atlas "cannot tow a boat-load of hysterical women a distance of one mile against wind, wave, and tide" or do any of the other amazing feats he claimed. The strongmen's struggle ended up before the Federal Trade Commission, which dismissed Hoffman's case against Atlas in 1937.

Atlas's program—and Mac's dilemma—remained unchanged for half a century and was further vindicated by the compliment of imitation. During the 1960s, Dynamic Tension began a second life as America's exercise fad of the decade, under a new, more technical, name: isometrics. But many still preferred the old way chosen by poor Mac. When Charles Atlas died on Christmas Eve of 1972 at the age of 80, he was still receiving 70,000 requests a year for the secrets of the world's most famous former weakling. □

Volks Gym

When turn-of-the-20th-century city dwellers found themselves getting flabby for lack of outdoor exercise, one solution was the German Heilgymnastik, or "Health Gymnasium," an assortment of early exercise equipment that prefigures the muscle-building machines used today. Among the eight Heilgymnastik designs were a calf stretcher *(above),* an arm strengthener *(right),* and an elaborately counterweighted device *(below)* used for arm bends.

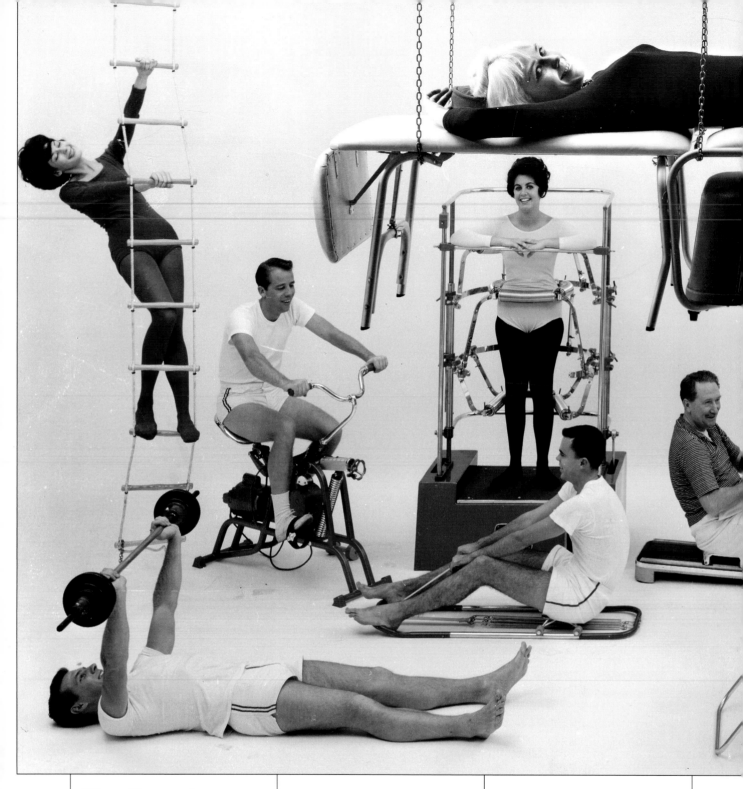

No Sweat

Life was once sufficiently strenuous to keep the body in reasonable trim. With the advent of the Industrial Age, however, millions of peo- ple were lured by the relative ease of city living. By the 1890s the machine age was offering a solu- tion for the ensuing flabbiness: engines of exercise that helped the flabby work their way to fitness.

Although most of the 1960s- vintage models shown here were only variations on that theme, some modern devices added a twist: They required no physical exertion whatever. A svelte figure

could be created by the flick of a switch. For example, the user of the Figurama oscillating table *(center, top)* had only to recline while the table supposedly vibrated excess flesh away. The motorized Slendro Ring Roller *(center, left)* offered to knead unwanted flabby flesh to firmness with electrically powered rollers. The Roaler Massager *(center, far right)* was billed as toughening stomach muscles with an arch of metal rolling pins. And for those who wanted to work up a sweat, there was also the portable plastic tent of the Streamline steam bath *(center, right)*. □

Air Breathers

Growing up in Oklahoma City, Ken Cooper had been a track star in high school, one of those slender young men whose training and genetic heritage enable them to add strength and stamina to a featherweight frame. But after graduation, Cooper turned his attention from athletics to his studies in college and medical school and later to his budding medical career in Texas and the U.S. Air Force. When he completed his schooling in 1956, the 29-year-old Cooper weighed 195 pounds, 30 pounds more than his high-school running weight, and his strength and stamina had deserted him—an unpleasant fact that he discovered one day while water-skiing. After only three minutes on the water, Cooper collapsed. "I was so out of condition that I nearly passed out from exhaustion, and I did throw up," he said later.

Cooper's unpleasant aquatic experience turned out to have happened to the right person at the right time. After entering the air force in 1960, Cooper was assigned to the School of Aerospace Medicine near San Antonio and began a study that would ultimately help him retrieve his fitness—and provide enhanced fitness for millions of others as well. As he tested the endurance of air-force men and women, Cooper noted that his volunteer subjects, presumed to be paragons of health, were actually in no better shape than he. More research convinced him that only one in five Americans could be called fit, at least by his lights.

The air-force medic's litmus test for fitness was the rate of oxygen consumption during exercise. A person who uses more oxygen is converting food into energy more efficiently than one who uses less, and this heightened efficiency translates into greater fitness. Cooper concluded that the unfit heart and lungs could be strengthened and conditioned to work more efficiently by subjecting them to sustained strenuous effort. He called this kind of training aerobic, after the Greek terms for "living in air." Running and jogging were the most aerobically demanding, Cooper reckoned, followed by swimming, bicycling, racquet and court sports, and walking.

Cooper published his exercise program, called simply *Aerobics*, in 1968. It sold two million copies in less than three years, spawned a craze for jogging, and made aerobics a household word. Cooper went on to found an $11-million fitness research center in suburban Dallas and is proud of the fact that deaths from heart disease dropped 14 percent during the 1970s—he feels that *Aerobics* helped to bring about the change.

It was inevitable that something so popular would escape from the domain of medicine into the larger world. A few years after Cooper's publication, aerobic exercise was being promoted not merely as a way to health, but as a route to beauty—and a way of life. One populariz-er was Judi Shep-pard Missett, who blended jazz dance and calisthenics in her 1978 book *Jazzercize: A Fun Way to Fitness.* "Energy is a source of sheer

Father of the aero-bics movement, physician Ken Coo-per competes in the annual Tyler Cup marathon in Dal-las, Texas.

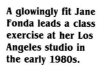

A glowingly fit Jane Fonda leads a class exercise at her Los Angeles studio in the early 1980s.

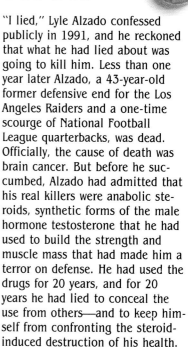

delity," was the volume's epigraph, quoting the German philosopher and student of power Friedrich Wilhelm Nietzsche. "The sedentary life," Nietzsche had written, "is the real *sin* against the holy spirit."

Perhaps the brightest star in the aerobic-fitness firmament is actress Jane Fonda, whose desire to invest proceeds from her stage and screen career led to the founding of her Workout aerobics studio in Beverly Hills, California, in 1979. Under the guidance of the lithe actress, aerobics became far removed from its staid military origins and outjazzed Jazzercize. Fonda's workout was no reflective jog around the track or graceful moves to the easy rhythms of modern music. Hers was hard work, done

to a pulsing rock beat in space-age costumes. Out went unattractive baggy shorts and sweatsuits, and in came form-fitting spandex, which made even ordinary bodies look good.

The combination of Hollywood glamour and the promise of a tight, youthful figure proved compelling to millions of women who followed Fonda's injunction to "feel the burn" of muscle strain. *Jane Fonda's Workout* in book, audiotape, and video formats rolled up some two million dollars in annual sales during its first few years; sequels included workouts for older and pregnant women. Colorful, flattering exercise clothing followed. The fitness explosion transformed Fonda's own image. Formerly viewed as a screen star turned political activist, she was named the third most influential woman in America in the 1984 *World Almanac*, behind First Lady Nancy Reagan and Supreme Court justice Sandra Day O'Connor. Now a fit 50-plus, Fonda is less active in her business, but her Workout programs remain popular. Jazzercize also flourishes, with some 4,700 instructors worldwide, and a host of celebrities offer competing aerobics schemes in what has become a huge market. Tights, leotards, and other accouterments of aerobics classes are fashionable street wear, and the sleek, resilient body has become the ideal for the millennium. □

A Drug to Die For

"I lied," Lyle Alzado confessed publicly in 1991, and he reckoned that what he had lied about was going to kill him. Less than one year later Alzado, a 43-year-old former defensive end for the Los Angeles Raiders and a one-time scourge of National Football League quarterbacks, was dead. Officially, the cause of death was brain cancer. But before he succumbed, Alzado had admitted that his real killers were anabolic steroids, synthetic forms of the male hormone testosterone that he had used to build the strength and muscle mass that had made him a terror on defense. He had used the drugs for 20 years, and for 20 years he had lied to conceal the use from others—and to keep himself from confronting the steroid-induced destruction of his health.

A high-school All-American football player from Cedarhurst, New York, Lyle Alzado graduated with great expectations for a college and professional sports career. But, although he was a rangy six feet three inches tall and weighed in at 190 pounds, Alzado was too small to make the cut at a major university. Only one college would accept him into its football program, tiny Yankton College in South Dakota, and even there, Alzado learned that his relatively small size tended to keep him on the bench. Disappointed, Alzado sought and found a miracle to salvage his athletic ambitions: anabolic steroids.

Buying the drug Dianabol at a local gym and ingesting 50 milligrams daily, Alzado put on mus- ◊

cle as fast as he could lift weights. The dimensions of his arms and legs grew dramatically within a few weeks. His weight shot up, eventually reaching almost 300 pounds. But he was not just bigger and stronger—he was meaner. Alzado was a victim of what steroid users call " 'roid rages"—psychotic delusions of grandeur, hallucinations, paranoia, depression, and mania. His opponents feared him. His coaches loved him, as did professional scouts.

The Denver Broncos drafted Alzado in 1971, and he continued using steroids in order to maintain his place in a profession where large, dangerously aggressive athletes competed for fame and glory. He was rewarded in 1977 by being named the National Football League's Defensive Player of the Year. Alzado credited the drugs. "I saw that the steroids made me play better and better," he said. "I kept on because I knew I had to keep getting more size."

In 1982 Alzado joined the Raiders—and his steroid use increased. After a decade in professional sports, he had begun to feel that his position was threatened by younger and stronger athletes; his "miracle drug" was the only way he had to keep up. "I just didn't feel strong unless I was taking something," he said later. Most steroid

users ingest the drugs in cycles. After several weeks of use, the doses begin to lose their effect, so the athletes give their bodies a rest before starting up again. Alzado never paused, instead moving from one type of steroid to another. "I'd feel my body close up on one drug and I'd switch to another until my body would open up to the first one again." At one point, Alzado was spending between $20,000 and $30,000 a year on steroids.

But the warning signs were there, and ultimately Alzado could no longer ignore them. Plastic surgery was needed to remove

lumps that formed under the skin of his buttocks, where he injected the drugs. In one operation, the doctor removed one baseball-size mass of tissue, only to find a larger one under it. And Alzado's rages made him fearsome off the field as well as on. "I did things only crazy people do," he said later. "Once in 1979 in Denver a guy sideswiped my car, and I chased him up and down hills through the neighborhoods. I did that a lot. I'd chase a guy, pull him out of his car, beat the hell out of him."

By 1985 not even drugs could keep Alzado on top, and an injury

Practicing wheelbarrow push-ups on a California beach, 264-pound Lyle Alzado trains with his physician for a 1990 comeback attempt. The ailing football pro later revealed that he had augmented his size and strength by taking steroids *(top)* and growth hormones.

to his Achilles tendon forced him to retire after 14 years in professional football. Retirement, however, did not end Alzado's addiction to steroids. He now had a budding movie career that demanded he maintain his physique. Nor could he stand, as he put it, "the thought of being weak"—or, as it turned out, the thought of being away from football. In 1990, at the age of 41, Lyle Alzado decided to make a comeback with the Raiders. He began daily workouts with a squad of trainers—and a cabinet full of drugs. This time Alzado added a newly available, genetically engineered human-growth hormone to his list of substances. He grew stronger, faster, and recovered quickly from a knee injury received in training. But the Raiders dropped Alzado after the season's first exhibition game.

Then Alzado's body began falling apart. He experienced dizziness, nausea, and fainting. He was in and out of the hospital, undergoing tests. Finally, in February 1991, he was diagnosed with cancer. According to Dr. Robert Huizenga, one of the physicians who treated Alzado, the rare T-cell lymphoma that invaded the athlete's once-invincible body was a direct result of using anabolic steroids and growth hormones—both can foster cancer.

Weak and bald from chemotherapy and shrunken in size, Alzado spent the next year telling his cautionary story of steroid use. "If what I've become doesn't scare you off steroids," he told his audiences, "nothing will." That year was all he had left. On May 14, 1992, the 43-year-old defensive end once called the "apotheosis of ferocity" died in Portland, Oregon. □

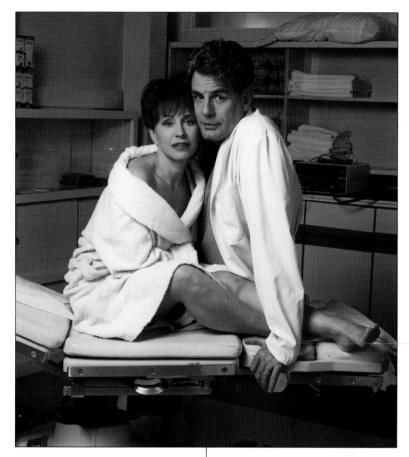

Perfect Match

When Harvey Austin says his wife is beautiful, as he often does, it is difficult to know whether he is really talking about her or his own handiwork. Austin is a plastic surgeon, and his wife, Carol, is one of his best customers, having undergone 13 operations at his hands.

Although surgeons have traditionally avoided operating on family members, Austin is just one of a growing number of cosmetic surgeons who practice what they preach on their nearest and dearest. There is nothing wrong with playing Pygmalion at home, says

Plastic surgeon Harvey Austin snuggles with wife and perennial patient Carol on an operating table in his Virginia office.

Austin: "Who better to operate on you than someone who loves you?"

The Austins broke the surgical ice in 1980, when Carol, then 35, complained about puffy skin around her eyes. Harvey offered to fix the problem with a lower eye lift, a procedure in which excess skin and pads of fat below the ◊

eyes are removed and the incisions hidden by skillful suturing. Before the operation, Carol Austin admits, she was just as apprehensive as any other patient. But afterward, she was sold. "Once you've gone through the fear of having it done the first time," she says, "it's okay to do everything else."

Everything else has been a nose job to straighten the bridge; a cheek lift and implants to provide movie-star cheekbones; liposuction to remove excess fat from chin, hips, and thighs; a tummy tuck to flatten out a midsection; a bra lift to reverse the effects of time and gravity on her bust; a corner mouth lift to add lilt to her smile; and "touch-up" suction to improve the shape of her knees and inner thighs. Her husband has done this, and more—for he also visits the surgical fountain of youth.

In fact, Harvey Austin is a living affirmation of his profession, having had his face, eyes, mouth, and neck lifted, his tummy tucked, fat removed by liposuction, and his skin smoothed by dermabrasion, a technique of gently sanding away rough patches and scar tissue caused by acne or injury. Lacking a surgeon-spouse, Harvey has had to rely on professional colleagues outside the family.

Between them, the Austins have undergone 20 procedures in a dozen years of marriage. Harvey says that they underwent surgery simply as a form of self-improvement—so they could look as good on the outside as they felt on the inside. Carol agrees. "I'm not a movie star," she modestly admits. "I'm not unbelievably gorgeous." In the view of this striking couple, cosmetic surgery is its own reward; vanity has nothing to do with it. □

Flowery Toes

"I wept and hid in a neighbor's home, but mother found me, scolded me, and dragged me home. She shut the bedroom door, boiled water, and from a box withdrew binding, shoes, knife, needle and thread." The speaker, a woman born into a traditional family that lived near Shanghai, was recalling a terrifying moment in her girlhood. Like millions of other young Chinese females before her, she had been about to undergo the ritual of foot-binding, a 1,000-year-old rite of passage that crippled girls in the cause of an ancient notion of beauty.

Her mother, she continued, trimmed the seven-year-old's toenails, washed her feet, and began to wrap each in 10-foot-long strips of cloth a mere two inches wide. She turned her daughter's four smaller toes under, forcing them into the sole of her foot, and continued wrapping and tightening the cloths. When she finished, she sewed the bindings tight. The task complete, the mother announced, "Today is a lucky day. If bound today, your feet will never hurt; if bound tomorrow, they will." But the little girl's feet did hurt; sometimes the pain was so excruciating that she sobbed every time she tried to walk. Gradually her feet stopped bleeding, and pain faded into numbness. After two years, the procedure was pronounced a success. The girl's feet, no more than three inches long, were permanently folded in upon themselves. To Western eyes they were considered disfigured; but traditional Chinese deemed them beautiful.

Although her youthful agonies were great, the Shanghai woman—

one of the last to have her feet bound in that fashion—did survive them. Others were not so fortunate: The narrow, tightly wrapped bandages sometimes cut off the flow of blood, causing gangrene and fatal infection. Loss of toes was common, and nerve damage was the rule; after two years of pain, all sensation died.

According to most accounts, the practice began when noblewomen decided to emulate court dancers during the ninth-century Tang dynasty. The dancers bound their feet when enacting the story of an Indian princess whose feet were tiny and delicate, like a doe's, and whose footprints resembled lotus flowers, a symbol of fecundity. Other well-to-do ladies soon followed the fashion for "lotus" feet, binding them ever more tightly and slipping them into tiny red satin shoes, the better to contrast with their ivory skin. The smaller the feet, the greater their beauty.

The discipline of foot-binding later spread throughout the social classes and was widely regarded as a mark of refinement. Bound feet became objects of erotic fancy, to be unbound only in the boudoir; to catch a glimpse of a beloved's naked foot was thought to be bliss. The knowledgeable worshiper nibbled watermelon seeds and almonds from between his lover's contorted toes and caressed the stunted feet while making love. Sex manuals devoted many pages to the proper way to hold a foot. The Manchu emperors of the 17th and 18th centuries tried and failed to outlaw foot-binding, which had its practical side as well: A maiden could not hope to land a husband with the ugly feet of the unbound.

In the social upheaval following

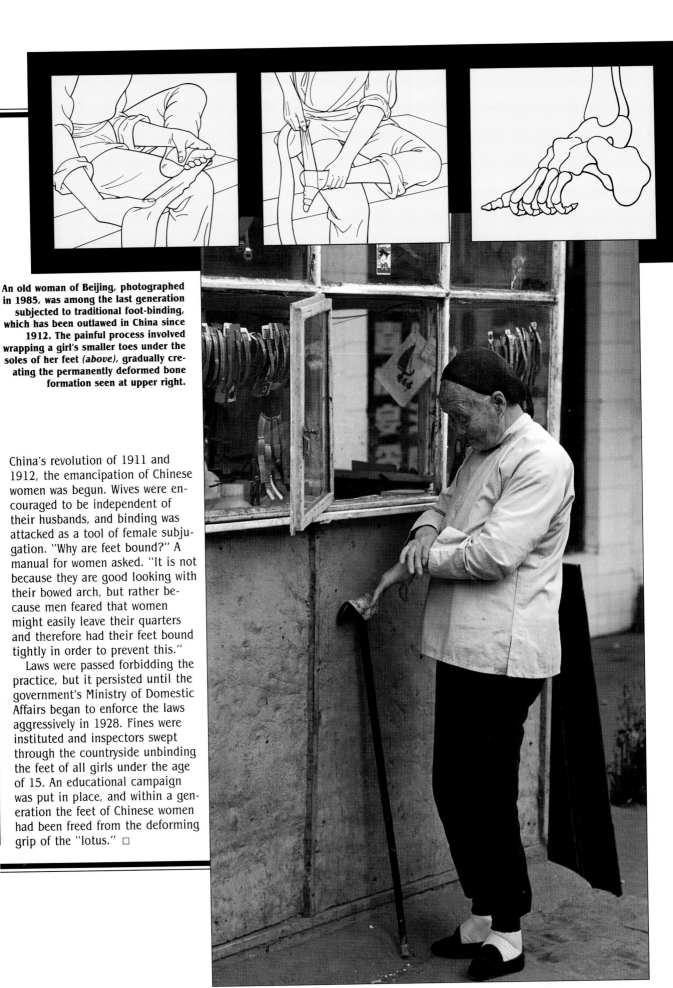

An old woman of Beijing, photographed in 1985, was among the last generation subjected to traditional foot-binding, which has been outlawed in China since 1912. The painful process involved wrapping a girl's smaller toes under the soles of her feet *(above)*, gradually creating the permanently deformed bone formation seen at upper right.

China's revolution of 1911 and 1912, the emancipation of Chinese women was begun. Wives were encouraged to be independent of their husbands, and binding was attacked as a tool of female subjugation. "Why are feet bound?" A manual for women asked. "It is not because they are good looking with their bowed arch, but rather because men feared that women might easily leave their quarters and therefore had their feet bound tightly in order to prevent this."

Laws were passed forbidding the practice, but it persisted until the government's Ministry of Domestic Affairs began to enforce the laws aggressively in 1928. Fines were instituted and inspectors swept through the countryside unbinding the feet of all girls under the age of 15. An educational campaign was put in place, and within a generation the feet of Chinese women had been freed from the deforming grip of the "lotus." □

Chewing the Fat

Horace Fletcher, a wealthy San Francisco manufacturer and importer, was appalled one day in 1895 when an insurance company turned down his application for life insurance. Fletcher had thought he was in good health, but the company thought otherwise. Given his height of five feet, seven inches, and weight of 217 pounds, Fletcher, the insurer opined, was too fat.

Fletcher tried to lose weight for three years. He fasted and exercised, to no effect. So great was his frustration that he even considered entering medical school to search for a solution to his intractable weight problem. Then, disappointed by every common reducing regimen he could find, Fletcher tried something he had seen from time to time among the recommendations of nutrition gurus— the thorough chewing of all food.

"Industrious munching," as Fletcher called it, involved chewing at a constant rate of 100 munches per minute. Depending on its consistency, every mouthful of food was crunched between 30 and 70 times, although very fibrous foods, such as shallots, could require as long as seven minutes, or 700 munches. Even milk and soup had to be chewed, or dyspepsia would surely result. According to some of the earlier advocates, such thorough mastication helped reduce weight by thoroughly breaking down food particles in preparation for digestion. The more skeptical said all the chewing simply consumed so much time that people could not eat as much as they ordinarily would. Whatever the truth, within four months of starting to chew his food more thoroughly, Fletcher had slimmed down to 163 pounds, a weight he maintained for the rest of his life.

Having proved the value of mastication in his own life, Fletcher became its missionary. Chewing, Fletcher claimed, could transform "a pitiable glutton into an intelligent Epicurean." He stumped the country preaching the values of Fletcherizing, as it was soon called. "Nature will castigate those who don't masticate," he threatened, and before long, Fletcherism had captivated turn-of-the-century America, a land obsessed with self-improvement.

Inevitably, health became a secondary goal of the Fletcherites. Slender beauty was the real objective, and slimness— as achievable through Fletcherism—was linked with financial and social success. Prolonged chewing became de rigueur at the dinner tables of the fashionably

Wearing his customary white suit, dapper chewing enthusiast Horace Fletcher was photographed for his 1913 book, *Fletcherism*.

healthy. Both great and humble embraced it. By 1910 John D. Rockefeller, novelist Henry James, and inmates of Sing Sing Prison all enthusiastically practiced Fletcherism. The white-garbed, optimistic Fletcher became a pied piper, leading the novelty-hungry press to such heartwarming stories as that of the students of Miss Palmer's kindergarten in Buffalo, New York, who solemnly devoted 20 minutes each day to the chewing of a single cracker. In 1913 Fletcher published a best-selling book, *Fletcherism: What It Is, or, How I Became Young at Sixty*, and during World War I served as food economist of the Committee for Relief in Belgium. He died of bronchitis in Copenhagen, Denmark, on January 13, 1919, at age 69.

Fletcherism may have been the first of a long line of weight-reduction programs and products that appeared through the 20th century. In the 1920s the influence of the Fletcherites converged with the growing popularity of exercise for its own sake and the newly slim, curve-free line favored by fashion illustrators, who spurred Americans toward an ideal of slimness that was neither natural nor easily attainable. Many perceived a link between waistlines and wealth, summed up a generation later by an aphorism attributed to socialite Babe Paly: "You can never be too thin or too rich."

But the quest for less was also aided and abetted by Horace Fletcher's old nemesis, the insurance companies, and their frustrating statistics. Despite those years of heavy chewing, actuarial tables published in 1924 labeled as "overweight" half of all Americans over 35 years old. □

Sheepish Youth

Paul Niehans *(below)*, a German surgeon living in Switzerland during the 1920s, claimed to be the illegitimate son of Kaiser Wilhelm. The distinction—neither confirmed nor denied by the royal family—earned Niehans a clientele dotted with the names of Europe's wealthy and noble. But what made him rich was his claim that he possessed the secrets of eternal youth and applied them at the famous Swiss spa Clinic La Prairie.

Since the late 1800s, wealthy, aging Europeans had been receiving transplanted tissue from the reproductive organs and other glands of simians, in a misguided and dangerous effort to restore virility. The treatment was worse than worthless; patients suffered from infections, tissue rejection, and simian syphilis. Nevertheless, the practice persisted, capitalizing on a mistaken belief, common to folk medicine around the world, that animal organs have special properties when transferred to humans.

In the 1920s and 1930s, Niehans extended the concept with what he called cellular therapy—the injection into humans of ground-up cells from a sheep fetus. The treatment, he claimed, was good for a variety of ailments and was capable of rejuvenating aging bodies. By infusing tired old cells with frisky young ones from unborn animals, he claimed to have caused a dwarf to grow more than 12 inches and to have saved a woman whose par-

athyroid gland had been destroyed.

But it was not until after World War II that Niehans managed to institutionalize his restorative works. In 1948 he joined the staff of Clinic La Prairie, on the shores of Lake Geneva in Montreaux, and under his influence, La Prairie was transformed from an out-of-the-way infirmary to a posh retreat for the wealthy, attracted by Niehans's claimed cure. Cellular therapy, Niehans assured his clients, was an antidote to cancer, birth traumas, mental retardation, dandruff, and "executive diseases." After undergoing tests to determine which of their organs were flagging, La Prairie's clients received multiple sheep-cell injections, then were confined to bed for several days. They were released after a week ◊

Generations of celebrity patients have been drawn to Clinic La Prairie *(above)* on Switzerland's Lake Geneva by the spa's famed cellular therapy, in which a substance *(far left)* made from minced sheep fetuses *(near left)* is said to rejuvenate tired human beings—a claim not yet verified by science.

but cautioned to avoid the cell-damaging effects of x-rays, saunas, and very hot hair dryers.

The rich and famous responded with enthusiasm. The duke and duchess of Windsor, screen stars Gloria Swanson and Charlie Chaplin, political leaders Winston Churchill and Charles de Gaulle, and author Somerset Maugham were among the prominent multitude that flocked to Montreaux, followed by a bevy of less well-known business leaders, sheiks, and pashas. Each paid $2,500 for the week-long treatment.

La Prairie's prime physician was happy to make house calls—at least for some clients. In 1954 Niehans flew to the Vatican, where he treated 77-year-old Pope Pius

XII for a stomach complaint with a shipment of freeze-dried sheep fetus cells. Doctors throughout Europe rushed to imitate Neihans's formula. No matter that research failed to confirm the efficacy of cellular therapy. An American Medical Association study in the 1960s failed to find any benefit in it, although the intruding cells did produce some increase in immune-system functions.

Niehans claimed that cellular therapy had cured him of a prostate condition in 1949, but it could not save him from the ultimate malady—old age. He died in 1971 at the age of 87. The doctor's legacy continues to propel Clinic La Prairie, however. Its brochure proclaims that "aged cells,

after exposure to Clinic La Prairie's purified concentrate, can regain and express properties that, in the course of aging, were temporarily lost." In 1992 the basic one-week cure cost $7,500.

The original, 24-bed La Prairie facility still stands and still accommodates cell-therapy patients. For another $5,000 a week, guests can be pampered in a modern 42-bed complex that features fitness, exercise, and diet regimens, including such therapies as ozone showers and "corpofit," a technique for removing fat and wrinkles electrically. And, for those who are not sheepish about looking as young as La Prairie has made them feel, the clinic has added plastic surgery. □

IMPROVING ON NATURE

Whether nature has been generous or stingy with its gifts, humans are loath to leave their natural endowments unimproved. The beautiful and the plain alike find themselves enhanced—and their spirits lifted—by an added dab of color, the sparkle of a gem, or, when the cultural climate is right, the insertion of a polished nose bone or lip plate of tinted clay. Often, however, the preferred site is the hair, which grows rapidly and comes in various textures and hues. Stalking the protean models of length, color, and curl, coiffures range wildly from modest caps to towering absurdities, worn on bodies rendered fashionably hairless or kept stylishly furred.

Hirsute or bare, skin is the canvas on which cosmetics draw the momentary face of beauty. The ghostly white-lead masks of highborn Roman and Elizabethan women were once loveliness itself, as the scars and perforations worn by some modern tribes are beautiful to others now. But decoration serves more than vanity. It also binds the outcast denizens of the nether world with irrevocable badges of membership: whole suits of illustrated skin, secret penetrations of the body, insignias of scars. Intoxicated with the wine of fashion, or the stronger stuff that cements groups of peers, humans can find beauty anywhere.

A 4,500-year-old limestone figure of an Egyptian scribe *(below)*, excavated in 1893, shows the green-lined eyes of his day. At right, a frieze of banqueting women wear fragrantly scented cones of grease atop their stiff black wigs.

Eyeliners

Although 12,000-year-old shards of paint palettes and other cosmetic utensils have been discovered in northern Africa, the first detailed record of personal adornment comes from the epoch of the Egyptian pharaohs, which began some 5,000 years ago. The slender golden faces that survive only as busts and paintings were as striking then as they are today and widely imitated—especially their bold exaggeration of the eye. Men and women alike applied shiny, dark streaks of kohl, a paste of water or saliva and such compounds as powdered lead, antimony, and magnesium oxide to their upper lids and for an inch or so beyond the eyes' outer edge. Their lower lids were smeared with malachite, a green copper ore.

As clearly decorative as the practice was, it appears to have had a therapeutic, as well as a cosmetic, origin. Like the "eye black" smears on the cheeks of modern athletes, the dark colors rimming ancient Egyptian eyes diminished the intense glare of the sun. The chemistry of the paint also benefited the wearer by repelling flies and by medicating eye diseases endemic to the area. Until the mid-20th century, for example, copper sulfate was the medicine of choice against trachoma, an infectious eyelid disease.

But the striking eye markings were barely the tip of ancient Egyptian cosmetics, which had a counterpart for virtually everything found on modern dressing tables: Paints, polishes, perfumes, lotions, mirrors, toilette boxes, razors, and manicure tools were all in the ar-

senal of beautification. Both sexes spread the equivalent of foundation makeup onto their faces, necks, chests, and upper arms. Men used yellow tints but could also use shades of orange. Women could employ only yellow hues, which they embellished by accenting the veining in their temples and breasts with a tracery of blue paint and sometimes with nipples painted gold.

Women frowned on wrinkles then, as they do now, and commonly applied overnight facial masks to tighten the skin and improve the complexion. One popular antiwrinkle formula included milk,

incense, wax, and olive oil; another included crocodile dung and juniper leaves. A wash for the complexion might include bullock's bile, whipped ostrich eggs, olive oil, flour, sea salt, resin, and fresh milk.

Body hair was considered dirty, and tweezers, pumice, razors, and *noorah*, a depilatory containing quicklime, were routinely used to remove it. Women shaved their eyebrows and redrew more dramatic curves with paints made of crocodile excrement, ass's liver, and opium, among other substances. Most men and women shaved their heads, partly for hygienic reasons and partly for religious ones. The shorn wore wigs, some crafted of

human hair, others of cotton wool or palm-leaf fibers woven in complex arrangements of braids and curls and not designed to appear natural. At large banquets, both guests and servants often topped their wigs with *bit*, conical mounds of myrrh-laden tallow. As the fat melted in the heat of the evening, it oozed down the shoulders in sticky streams, enveloping the throng in a cloud of intoxicating—and cooling—aroma.

In fact, many of the balms and body oils devised by Egyptian apothecaries were intended mainly to ease the effects of North Africa's desiccating heat. These early druggists expertly whisked together the spices and essences of Egypt and the Orient, including frankincense, myrrh, almonds, oil of roses, cinnamon, thyme, and marjoram, which they mixed with animal and vegetable fats.

The resulting unguents were not meant just for the aristocracy, however—even the lowest laborer was entitled to a ration of ointments. In what some historians believe was humankind's first strike, laborers working on the giant necropolis of Ramses III walked off the job when their ointment allotment was delayed. They and their noble masters were not the only ones to prize cosmetics highly: Precious cosmetic oils and creams placed in tombs for the use of the dead appear to have been as strong a magnet for grave-robbers as gold and gems. □

A naked servant carved in wood bears a makeup cup rimmed with lotus buds, Egypt's symbol of renewal.

Roman Games

Said to have been the most beautiful woman of her time, Poppaea Sabina may be less famous for inducing her lover and husband—the emperor Nero Claudius Caesar Drusus Germanicus—to kill his mother and his wife than for her self-indulgence. A twice-married blonde when she attracted the 21-year-old emperor in AD 58, Poppaea was said to require 100 servants to bathe, beautify, and dress her, and a stable of 500 gold-shod asses to supply the milk in which she took her daily baths. So closely was she linked with beauty that certain creams and unguents were named for her. On the royal scene only briefly—she died in AD 65 from a kick delivered by an angry Nero—Poppaea left more than a trail of intrigue and cruelty. To many she exemplifies a world obsessed with personal presentation.

In fact, Poppaea's voracious interest in baths, raiment, jewels, coiffure, and cosmetics was only an extreme example of the practices of every Roman who could afford it. Although few were able to match the labor-intensive hygiene of the imperial household, the free citizens of Rome evidently spent more waking hours engaged in the rituals of cleansing and beautification than any other European people before or since.

Romans gathered each day in public baths, usually in the afternoon so they could soak and steam away the day's cares and perfume themselves for the evening. Even the wealthy, who possessed private baths, often preferred the clubby sociability of the public baths, which were open to both men and

In a bas-relief from the second century AD, servant girls aid their lady's elaborate toilette *(above)*. At right, a statue of a Roman girl wears the heaped curls of the popular *orbis* hair style.

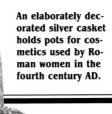

An elaborately decorated silver casket holds pots for cosmetics used by Roman women in the fourth century AD.

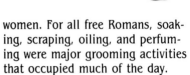

women. For all free Romans, soaking, scraping, oiling, and perfuming were major grooming activities that occupied much of the day.

The hair of aristocratic women was dyed, curled, waved, and pinned by hairdressers, called *ornatrices,* according to changing fashion. Hair styles were complex and ever changing. Among the most popular was the *orbis,* a concatenation of curls piled high on a wire frame. In the empire's capital, black, red, and blond hair dyes were popular among respectable women—the last despite the legal requirement that all prostitutes wear yellow hair. But the dyes were often caustic and caused baldness that had to be covered by a wig—preferably one made from the fair hair of the empire's Germanic and Gallic subjects. So obsessively important was hair fashion that women who were to be portrayed in sculpted busts sometimes demanded that the artist make the figure's hair detachable, so that it could be restyled as fashions changed.

Although most Roman women used far fewer servants than Nero's Poppaea, many relied on packs and potions to maintain their beauty. Face packs were put on at bedtime and were often made of sheep's fat and breadcrumbs, or perhaps crocodile excrement, eggs, barley, and honey. Other exotic potions, such as one that included kingfisher guano, were used to remove pimples and other facial blemishes.

Wealthy Romans employed slaves called *cosmetae* to apply depilatories and wield tweezers against stray hairs and to apply a fashionable foundation of white lead to face, neck, and arms. The highborn rouged their lips and cheeks with wine dregs or red ocher and accentuated their eyelids, lashes, and brows with ashes or antimony. Beautiful brows were those that met over the nose. A second team of slaves—the *parasitae*—were kept around to praise the cosmetic outcome.

Although pervasive, this Roman self-absorption was not universally admired. In *The Art of Love,* the first-century poet Ovid advised women: "On no account let your lover come upon you surrounded by the accoutrements of your cosmetic art. Your artifice should go unsuspected. Who could help but feel disgust at the thick paint on your face melting and running down onto your breasts?"

Two generations later, the Roman satirist Juvenal addressed this question to a compatriot:

"But tell me yet—this thing, thus daubed and oiled / Poulticed, plastered, baked by turns and boiled, / Thus with pomatums, ointments lacquered o'er, / Is it a face, Usidius, or a sore?" □

Death Mask

While on the prowl for a new wife, England's King Henry VII considered the recently widowed queen of Naples a likely prospect and queried emissaries who had actually met the woman as to "whether she be painted or not." Italians, he believed, had a particular reputation for gaudy self-decoration. Henry's men on the scene were happy to report back, "As far as we can perceive or know, that the said Queen is not painted." Evidently, her natural look was not enough, however, to compensate for her dearth of dowry.

But Henry was a man already out of his time, sartorially speaking. When his granddaughter took the throne as Queen Elizabeth I in 1559, female beauty had become a grand gown topped by a perfectly white face and bosom, with splashes of red on each cheek, and a crimson gash for a mouth.

In their quest for makeup to supply this garish bust, Elizabethan housewives and apothecaries relied on a variety of antique formulas, pounding ocher and cochineal to concoct rouge and lip crayons and mixing up *fucus,* a red paint usually applied to the lips, from ground jawbone of hog and poppy oil. The fashionable pallor was achieved by covering the face and bosom with ceruse—white lead—or bleaching with sulfur and borax. Such worrisome imperfections as freckles and acne could be erased with mixtures of citrus and powdered mercury, among other things. The entire ghostly face was lacquered with egg white.

As England came to rule the seas, British merchants added new, exotic ingredients from abroad: ◊

Her face and chest rendered pale by the application of white lead and other cosmetics, fashionable Lady Frances Fairfax sits for her 1610 portrait.

Myrrh and spices, musk, ambergris, jasmine, saffron, Venetian turpentine, and other rare substances found their way into Elizabethan dressing rooms in ointments and oils, and onto the pale visage so coveted by noble-women of the time. When the Elizabethan woman looked in her mirror—the sea trade had made these formerly rare devices accessible to nearly everyone—a stiff and unnatural reflection returned her gaze. Passersby were usually spared such a sight, however, for ladies further protected their carefully encased visages with cloth or leather masks, held in place with a strategically located button gripped by the teeth.

Thus disguised, wellborn Englishwomen confronted the filthy urban world of their day. The streets of cities and towns were little better than open sewers, and men and women alike carried nosegays or pomanders of perfumed paste to help diffuse the stench. Sweet odors were also thought to serve a medicinal purpose. Having no knowledge of microorganisms, Elizabethans believed disease could not flourish in the presence of pleasant scent.

The gentry also prized sweet breath and clean teeth and had numerous techniques for achieving both—abrasive cleaning compounds, toothpicks, and perfumed mouthwashes of wine, honey, herbs, and alum abounded. Despite such attentions, Elizabethan teeth were notably bad: The pursed lips on portraits often conceal decayed or missing teeth. In fact, personal hygiene in general left much to be desired—Elizabeth, like her subjects, bathed no more than once a month. Most people cleaned themselves by rubbing with a coarse cloth and daubing with waters scented with jasmine, honeysuckle, or other flowers. The noble female body was simply less important than its decorated outer shell.

Many still considered painting to be ungodly, a sin of vanity and pride, a badge of easy virtue. Moralists derided the era's "apish fashions and follies." A Puritan wrote to question the uprightness of women who "colour their faces with certain oyles, liquors, unguents and waters made to that end." The same critic fumed that those who wore makeup could not perceive "that their soules are thereby deformed, and they brought deeper into the displeasure and indignation of the Almighty." The common wisdom of righteousness held that purity could be found in country damsels, who were ostensibly free from their citified sisters' affectations.

Censured but not deterred, middle- and upper-class Englishwomen continued to follow the lead of their feisty queen, who became increasingly wed to artifice as she grew older. Ironically, the very elements used to create the white mask of eternal youth carried the seeds of accelerated aging.

Although ceruse and sublimate of mercury helped achieve the desired visual effect, they could be horribly destructive of a woman's face. White lead was a potent poison, manufactured by steeping bars of lead in vinegar or urine, then scraping off the ensuing white flakes. Ceruse caused open sores, baldness, mental deficiency, and other chronic symptoms of lead poisoning in both its makers and users. As for the powder called sublimate of mercury, the Italian Giovanni Paolo Lomazzo wrote: "Such women as use it about their face, have alwaies black teeth, standing far out of their gums like a Spanish mule; an offensive breath, with a face halfe scorched, and an uncleane complexion. All which proceede from the nature of sublimate. So that simple women thinking to grow more beautifull, become disfigured, hastening olde age before the time."

If Elizabethan women knew of such penalties, they evidently ignored them. Perhaps, in a world where life tended to be short and health fleeting, one's physical well-being was less compelling than momentary beauty. □

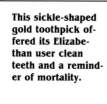

This sickle-shaped gold toothpick offered its Elizabethan user clean teeth and a reminder of mortality.

Patchwork

Lozenges and crescent moons, stars and circles, hearts and horse-drawn coaches: These were the adornments of the well-appointed visage in the 16th through 18th centuries. Cut from black velvet, silk, or paper-thin Spanish leather, patches—*mouches,* or "flies," as the French archly dubbed them—had a long reign as a preferred beauty aid of both sexes.

Although beauty patches were used by the noblewomen of ancient Rome, their use had declined during the austere centuries of the Middle Ages. With the renaissance in Italy, however, the black spots began to reappear, worn to evoke the *moticella,* or "birthmark," of Venus, the Roman goddess of love. Patches were fully revived by the style-conscious men and women of Paris, where the mouche was first worn in the late 1500s. From La Perle des Mouches, a chic shop in the rue St. Denis, the vogue spread through the fashionable circles of continental Europe; by the mid-1600s it had captured Britain.

Applied with gum mastic, a sticky elastic tree sap, the small pieces of material were often used to hide blemishes, disfiguring pits from a variety of poxes, or minor lesions caused by syphilis and other pervasive ailments of the day. As one wag wrote of a lady: "Her patches are of every cut / For pimples and for scars."

Apart from their masking function, patches also served to convey a host of romantic messages, which by the early 18th century had become codified into a silent language. Placement was the key to this amorous semaphore. A patch positioned near the mouth indicated a willingness to flirt; placed at the corner of the eye, a spot denoted burning desire. If a woman wore a patch on her right cheek, she signaled that she was married, if on her left cheek, that she was betrothed. Carrying a supply of

In this 18th-century engraving, a Frenchwoman applies patches carried in a compact patch box like the one at left.

patches and adhesive in slim, mirrored boxes—the precursors of modern compacts—elegantly crafted from silver, ivory, porcelain, or tortoise shell, a woman could change her spots at whim. Not only could she modulate the attentions of potential lovers as the situation dictated—she could also hide emerging zits.

At the height of the patching craze in England, this language ◊

acquired a political dimension as well. Those siding with the Whigs patched exclusively on the right, while Tory sympathizers limited themselves to the left. The importance of patching was such that at least one bride-to-be stipulated in her prenuptial agreement that after her marriage she would be at liberty to patch as she pleased, politically and otherwise, without interference from her husband.

Patching among men was mainly for dandies, who lived for fashion. "Look, you, signor," admonished a character in a 1640 play, *Lady's*

Privilege, "if't be a lover's part you are to act, take a black spot or two. I can furnish you; 'twill make your face more amourous and appear more gracious in your mistress' eyes." Grace aside, patches were believed to make wearers appear younger, although some observers found this approach could be overdone. Reported a late-17th-century tourist, "In England the young, old, handsome, ugly, are all bepatch'd till they are bed-rid. I have often counted fifteen Patches, or more, upon the Swarthy wrinkled phiz of an old Hag

three-score and ten and upwards."

Although the clergy reviled patches, as, indeed, they did all cosmetics, it was not moral rectitude that ultimately led Europeans to pull off their patches, but science. Edward Jenner's remarkable smallpox vaccine, introduced in 1796, undoubtedly reduced the incidence of pitting, which in turn caused the use of beauty spots to decline. In time, the real patch was replaced by a substitute, a discreet beauty mark that was applied not with mastic, but with a dark pencil. □

Beyond the Pale

Arsenic and its compounds have been a favorite tool of poisoners— real and imagined—for centuries. Yet despite the lethal reputation of the toxin, fashionable European and American women of the 1800s made a practice of nibbling the

poison. Their intention: not suicide, but a pale complexion.

During the Victorian era, the open use of cosmetics was frowned upon in polite society; only prostitutes, actresses, and other presumably less-respectable women applied powder and rouge in plain view of the world. The more genteel attempted other, less stigma-

tizing paths to pallor—they ate chalk and drank vinegar. In the 1830s, however, word reached the West that women in the Caucasus Mountains of central Russia— whose complexions were reputed to be marvelously clear and pale— attributed their skin tone to eating arsenic. The smooth-skinned, pal-

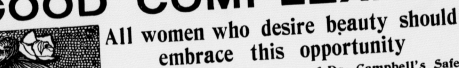

Max Factor's new cosmetic line, designed for use in films, flanks a photo of 1930s screen beauty Jean Harlow.

lid beauty described by visitors to the region became the envy of women in the salons of the West. Suddenly, arsenic was in.

Prepared in cream, liquid, or wafer form, arsenical products promising lustrous skin were advertised in magazines in the United States and abroad and were even carried by such prominent retailers as the Sears, Roebuck Company. Some doctors prescribed the toxic stuff. Fowler's Solution, an arsenic-based acne medication, was believed to impart a translucent look to the skin; women applied it as a face cream, which its manufacturers may not have intended. Arsenic Complexion Wafers, available in 40-cent and 75-cent sizes, were touted as "an excellent medicine for giving to the complexion a clearness and brilliancy not obtainable by external applications." They were also said to "improve the general health, causing the figure to grow plump and round."

The arsenic compounds did deliver the pale, anemic look, as promised—with health to match. The bluish tone that arsenic gave the skin was directly related to the element's toxic effect on red blood cells. With fewer red cells to carry oxygen to the body, arsenic consumers acquired the anemic hue that was then the rage. It is not known whether cosmetic arsenic killed any of its users, although the chronic anemia the substance produced evidently discouraged its use. By 1896 women were being advised to avoid arsenic-bearing products by a manual titled *Beauty: Its Attainment and Preservation.* But the real salvation came as makeup lost its stigma. Before long, even respectable ladies could be pale without being poisoned. □

Beauty Factor

Max Factor's career began and ended among the glamor and bright lights of show business. Born in Poland in 1875, he had begun his search for beauty by age 14, working as a wigmaker and theatrical makeup man in Russia's Imperial Grand Opera Company. At 20, Factor was a personal cosmetician to the czar's uncle, Alexander Nicolaivich Romanoff, to the czar's personal physicians, and to a crowd of lesser Russian nobility.

But in the first years of the 20th century, Factor was driven from Russia by a wave of virulent anti-Semitism and, like so many others, turned to the United States. Arriving in America in 1904, Factor went to St. Louis for a time, then, in 1908, moved to California, where he worked as a wigmaker and distributed the products of a cosmetics manufacturer. But the innovative immigrant soon unpacked his own cosmetics know-how as well and, in 1909, opened a small wig and cosmetic shop in downtown Los Angeles.

Seldom has the right person arrived in the right place so manifestly at the right time. Even as Factor opened his doors, the infant motion-picture business was in the process of relocating from cold, cloudy New York to sunny southern California; in 1907 the first film had been made there. Drawn to the new theatrical medium as he had been to the opera years earlier, Factor was soon turning out makeup to meet the fledgling industry's novel needs.

The first task was finding a replacement for the traditional thick grease paint used in the theater. This staple of the stage was unsuit-

able for filmmaking because it either melted or dried and cracked under the intensely hot movie lights. Forever fiddling with new compounds in his laboratory, Factor came up with a lighter, more flexible cream in 1914 and later packaged it in a compact, easy-to-carry tube. The product could be used on location, away from the comfort of studio dressing rooms.

Other innovations followed. Factor patented the eyebrow pencil in 1916. Soon human-hair eyelashes were added to the product line, then lip gloss, so that actresses need not lick their lips constantly to keep them moist and shiny. Because early black-and-white film did not render shades of gray accurately, Factor adjusted the colors and the light-absorption properties of his makeup so that the stars' faces looked natural onscreen. One formula, developed to suit the special needs of a new panchromatic film, earned Factor a special citation from the newly created Academy of Motion Picture Arts and Sciences in 1928. He also came up with a special makeup for television in 1932, when an early experimental station went on the air in Los Angeles.

That same year, Max Factor developed the beauty calibrator, a cruel-looking device used to measure facial proportions to within ◊

Encouraged by ads in such magazines as *Vogue (left),* turn-of-the-century beauties sought pallor by ingesting arsenic compounds.

a hundredth of an inch. Using it, Factor determined that not even the loveliest of Hollywood's stars measured up to ideal proportions. But by placing a shadow here and a highlight there he could create the appearance of perfection.

Factor was doing more than touching up the stars—he was training the rest of the world to imitate them. His name and products irrevocably linked with Hollywood's cinematic beauty, he fostered an unprecedented consumer demand for cosmetics. Canny businessman that he was, Factor used the entertainment industry for research and development. When a product proved successful there, it was then packaged and advertised for public consump-

MAX FACTOR
AND
CLARA BOW

tion. He was not shy about touting the popularity of his products with the stars; his makeup, he boasted, was so treasured by actresses that they filched it from their dressing rooms for use offscreen.

Through its special relationship with the studios, Factor's company was allowed to use movie-star endorsements in advertising, for a yearly fee of one dollar per star. At the grand opening of his newly renovated Hollywood headquarters in 1935—as lavish as any movie premiere, with 8,000 guests attending—the diminutive Factor stood on a stool as a parade of guests, including Judy Garland, Jean Harlow, Edward G. Robinson, and Claudette Colbert, posed with him for photos.

The master makeup man's last great invention came as motion pictures began the transition from black and white to Technicolor, which yielded glorious hues that audiences loved but was poor at rendering subtle skin tones. Worse, the panchromatic grease paint tended to absorb the bright colors of clothing and scenery, giving the actors and actresses blotchy, red and green faces. Factor countered in 1937 with Pan-Cake, a matte-finish cosmetic that could be applied quickly with a damp sponge. The makeup debuted in the film *Vogues of 1938*, starring Joan Bennett, and critics praised the natural look of the star.

Max Factor only just lived to see his Pan-Cake on the screen. He died later that year, aged 63, and like many of his famous clients, faded into Hollywood legend. □

Practicing what he preached, Max Factor makes up arch-flapper Clara Bow in the early 1920s, using cosmetics to achieve a perfection he was never able to find with his mechanical "beauty calibrator" (inset).

Toppers

Louis XIII, the melancholy 17th-century king of France, and Sun King Louis XIV, his extravagant heir, were vain prisoners of heredity: Both possessed a predisposition to premature baldness. Not surprisingly, their efforts to address the inherited flaw established a fashion that took 17th-century Europe by storm.

The royal pate of Louis *père* began to peek through the thinning, albeit resplendently long, regal hair while he was still in his twenties. Far too vain to settle for a crown of skin, Louis opted for a long mop of someone else's curly hair. His courtiers—ever considerate of the king's feelings—followed suit. By the time of Louis XIV's assumption of the throne in 1643, the wig had become standard issue for all who were sensitive to the current of fashion. Louis himself possessed a long, thick mane of natural hair until about the year 1672, when heredity began to overtake him. At first, the Sun King used a partial wig to cover his spreading bald spots, but finally he shaved his thinning locks and donned a full, flowing black wig—one of many products of his team of 40 wigmakers.

Across the English Channel, Puritan influence had maintained a close-cropped look until 1660. Then the restoration of Charles II to the Stuart throne revived a vogue of long male tresses. The wig followed in 1663, when Charles donned one to conceal his naturally graying locks.

Not everyone adopted the style immediately. Wigs remained controversial among the Puritan clergy, and in England and the colonies long hair and wigs were for a time abominated as a tool of the devil. Increase Mather, one of colonial America's most influential preachers and president of Harvard College, sermonized against them—but to little effect. By the early 18th century, churches were filled with wig-wearing communicants and preachers. Even Increase's son, the widely respected Cotton Mather, himself a wig wearer, preached vehemently against wig haters who, he charged, "strained at a gnat and swallowed a camel."

Mather adopted a stylish full-bottom wig, a solemn style—worn by men of property and judges—in which a mass of heavy curls cascaded over the shoulders like a shawl. Other designs had also become associated with specific professions. Coachmen wore wigs described by one observer as "in imitation of the curled hair of a water-dog." Tradesmen were distinguished by the compact bob. Physicians favored a long ◊

French ruler Louis XIV adopted a wig of shoulder-length black curls to hide his baldness, igniting an aristocratic rage for wigs among his courtiers, who slavishly followed the Sun King's lead.

bob called the physical. Military officers wore bag wigs, or pigtail wigs, with such names as the brigadier or, after the 1706 Anglo-French battle, ramillies.

Usually woven of human hair, wigs were at various times curled, frizzed, or left straight. They could be short, with neatly tied queues at the back, and sometimes teased into masses of curls above the queue. Whatever their shape, virtually all wigs were oiled, powdered liberally, and combed publicly with great show. Naturally, a trade of *perruquiers* arose to design, compose, dress, and restore hairpieces.

A man about London or Paris might own several wigs, representing an investment of anywhere from £5 to £200 each. Wealthy men often bequeathed wigs to their heirs; among the working classes, a good wig was a prized perk of apprenticeship. In cities, thieves specialized in snatching wigs off the heads of prosperous passersby. The thrifty might parlay one wig into the appearance of two with the addition of an extra pigtail or two. For all who could afford it, a panoply of equipment and material was available to aid in the care of their hairpieces. Bellows were used to powder them; more than a pound of flour at a time might be heaped on the hair. Cloth masks, paper cones, and powdering jackets protected the wig wearer from the dust. Some of the grander homes featured rooms devoted to the powdering of wigs.

But the affectations of wiggery had also made the practice ripe for ridicule. In 1764 a group of privileged young men fresh from a sojourn in Italy formed the Macaroni Club in London, adopting as their marks effeminate manners, foppish clothing, and an 18-inch-high padded wig. The outlandish dress and behavior of the Macaronis drew the barbs of satirists as well as the envy of less fortunate young men—including that quintessential young colonial Yankee Doodle, who, by sticking a feather in his cap, hoped to emulate the hip young turks across the waters.

The heyday of this male fashion ended with the 18th century, the victim of the tax collector and a public backlash against excess. The fulcrum of change was wheat flour, both a staple food and the preferred powder for a well-tended wig. Pounds and pounds of the substance were heaped on the hairpieces of the rich. Yet throughout the 17th and 18th centuries, high food prices and shortages caused by drought and war had triggered periodic riots, in which the public objected vehemently to flour's being devoted to frivolity rather than nourishment. In France, the storming of the Bastille in 1789 wrote *fini* to such ostentation. The short hair of a new order replaced the wig of aristocracy. In England, the government of Prime Minister William Pitt saw an opportunity to do good while doing well. Capitalizing on the popular outcry, in 1795 it slapped a one-guinea per person annual license fee on the use of flour for wig powdering.

By the standards of 18th-century politics, this was a minor dustup, but wigs soon fell into disfavor, and short, natural hair again became the fashion. The costly hairpieces of the wealthy were relegated to secondhand markets, where they were sold for pennies to shopkeepers and housewives for use as mops and dustrags. Not everyone was freed from false curls: Servants continued to wear the fossil fashion well into the 19th century, and white wigs remain a fixture of British law courts to this day. □

Head Men

"Leonard is coming," exclaimed Madame de Genlis, a well-known Parisian writer of the day, in 1769. "He is coming, and he is king!" In fact, Louis XV was then the ruler of France. But Leonard Autier occupied a crucial niche at the fashion-conscious court: He was its premier hairdresser.

Although not the first *coiffeur*, Leonard may have been the most notable of his time. Under his guidance, and that of such predecessors as the great LeGros and Larseneur, the ladies of France vied to exceed one another in the creation of elaborate hairdos. The men who tended these locks were not mere arrangers—they were architects of extravagance, true designers. Their tools were those of the tailor and the builder. And their clientele was the cream of the aristocracy. Leonard's clients, for example, included Madame du Barry, Louis XV's renowned mistress, and for 15 years he served the artfully extravagant Marie-Antoinette, wife of Louis XVI.

The creations of such artists were vast complexes of hair, stretched over wire armatures or felt pads, augmented by wads of horsehair, cotton wool, straw, and hemp, slathered with greasy pomades, and dusted with a finishing coat—often a pastel hue—of starch or flour. Truly fashionable ladies' hair sometimes rose nearly a yard, and perhaps twice that if topped with bobbing ostrich plumes or other, even more elaborate ornamentation.

Although the art of hair soon crossed the English Channel to London, its origins and apotheosis were French. The vogue evidently began in about 1680 with a makeshift bit of frippery devised by the duchesse de Fontanges, a paramour of Louis XIV's. After losing her hat during a royal hunt, she had tied up her curls with a lace-edged garter. Before long, women of the realm had embarked on a frenzy of imitation, elaborating upon Fontanges's approach with the addition of flocks of bows, ruffles, and lace. While most of them were coiffed by personal attendants, the demand for ever more complex hair styles firmly established the professional hairdresser.

The extent of this complexity was suggested by the English magazine *Connoisseur* in 1756. It described a design that featured a scale model of a coach fashioned from gold filament, "drawn by six dapple greys of blown glass, with a coachman, postilian, and gentleman within, of the same brittle manufacture." The man called LeGros, one of the world's first coiffeurs, published a textbook for his trade in 1765 that fueled the rage for big hair. By the 1770s women's hairdos had become grand constructions draped with pearls, jewels, and live flowers—the last sometimes kept fresh by hidden, water-filled receptacles molded to the curve of the skull. Menageries and cornucopias of fruits and vegetables were especially popular. As the vogue raged, the themes grew more and more exotic. Some arrangements included tableaus of miniature figures. Hot-air balloons swelled in mock ascent from coiffures, and in 1778 many a French head launched a frigate, in honor of a skirmish between the British *Arethusa* and France's *La Belle Poule*.

Naturally, the climb to the summit of fashion carried a price. Big hair was also big inconvenience. Sailing into salons in full regalia, women risked tangling with low-hanging chandeliers that blazed with candles. Occasionally, the hair confections caught fire. More often, there were rude encounters with doorways and coaches of insufficient height, requiring that women contort themselves to effect passage. Marie-Antoinette easily solved such transitory difficulties: She raised some of the doorways in Versailles and on at least one occasion had Leonard construct a hairdo in parts that could be disassembled for a carriage ride. Other noblewomen ◊

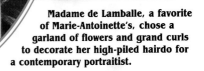

Madame de Lamballe, a favorite of Marie-Antoinette's, chose a garland of flowers and grand curls to decorate her high-piled hairdo for a contemporary portraitist.

followed suit. Eventually, some coach makers incorporated open tops in their vehicles or lowered the seats to accommodate the passengers' added stature. Even so, fashionably coiffed women had to kneel or stick their heads out carriage windows. At night, many ladies slept sitting up, in order to protect their giant dos.

But the constructions were not merely inconvenient—they were unhealthful. Once erected, a single hairdo might be worn for weeks, during which time the pomades and padding, all made of plant and animal derivatives, began to rot. Despite dosings with heavy perfumes, the hairdos were appallingly malodorous and worse—mites, lice, mice, and other vermin took up residence within.

France's bloody revolution in 1789 brought a gruesome end to the gargantuan fad: The towering coiffures never quite recovered from the guillotine's grim trimming. A survivor as well as an artist, Leonard managed to escape the revolution. When last seen, the king of hairdressers was appearing behind the crowned heads of Russia. □

Cartoonists roasted 18th-century hair styles in such exaggerated designs as a grandly horticultural one tended by a gardener *(left)* and a towering coiffure that, ignited by a blazing chandelier, has attracted a bucket brigade of firefighters.

Raging with Bristles

Joseph Palmer, a quiet, God-fearing butcher and produce merchant, moved to Fitchburg, Massachusetts, in 1830, where he so offended his fellow citizens that they continually jeered him, pelted him with clods and stones, and physically assaulted him. He was refused communion by his minister and finally jailed when he tried to defend himself from his attackers. Joseph Palmer's neighbors viewed him as "a human monster" and "un-American." It took about a year for Palmer to win his freedom.

Palmer's difficulties were just one example of the heat generated during the 19th-century debate over what some called pogonotrophy, a term derived from *pogon*, Greek for "beard." Although few men have suffered as materially as Palmer for the cultivation of a beard, those who preferred not to shave were subject to a long period of disapproval before they finally won the right to be hairy. To many respectable members of society, whiskers were a sign of insanity, religious fanaticism, or anarchy. Young radicals in France had taken to flaunting mustaches and beards during the 1830s, an affectation that soon became fodder for British satirists, who were ever alert to opportunities for tweaking their cross-Channel rivals. "When a party of young Frenchmen approach," quipped one Briton in 1844, "it is like the advance of a herd of goats."

Such witty criticism notwithstanding, the habit sprouted in Britain as well, partly because veterans returning from the Crimean War in the 1850s were loath to shave off the whiskers they had grown under fire. The debate over facial hair still raged in print, however. Opponents expressed disgust at the vulgarity of the excess hair and the moral laxity it must denote. Many businesses strictly prohibited the wearing of beards and mustaches—one firm reportedly asked its young male employees not to wear mustaches during business hours. Pro-beardists, on the other hand, extolled the aesthetic pleasures of whiskers as a male birthright and claimed that shaving was "a violation of hygienic law" that promoted diseases of the throat. Articles appeared contending that beards were items of "use, comfort, and ornament" and a salutory and "distinguishing characteristic of their sex." Eventually some Protestant clergymen even pronounced beards to be religiously correct.

In America, pogonics entered presidential politics in 1860. The president-elect, a craggy-faced, clean-shaven 51-year-old named Abraham Lincoln, had received some preelection advice. Eleven-year-old Grace Bedell of Westfield, New York, had told Lincoln he would look better with a beard. By the time of his inauguration the following March, Lincoln had sprouted the growth by which most now recognize him. En route by rail from Illinois to Washington, the president-elect bade the engineer stop in Westfield, where advance planners had made sure Lincoln's young adviser was waiting. ◊

Joseph Palmer's bearded visage peers from his tombstone, whose epitaph memorializes his struggle against prejudice.

Lincoln climbed down from his car, shook the girl's hand, and kissed her. "You see," he said, "I have let these whiskers grow for you, Grace."

Lincoln's acknowledgment made it into history books, and facial hair became as much the rule as the exception around the White House. Ulysses S. Grant, Rutherford B. Hayes, James Garfield, and Chester A. Arthur all subsequently took advantage of the precedent before the popularity of the fashion died out around the turn of the 20th century.

But Lincoln's trailblazing beard did little to ease the bad memories of Joseph Palmer. The Massa-chusetts butcher eventually befriended such luminaries as Ralph Waldo Emerson, Nathaniel Hawthorne, and Henry David Thoreau. When Palmer went to his grave in 1873, aged 84, his son Thomas marked the old man's tombstone with this bitterly understated reminder of the father's ordeal: "Persecuted for wearing the beard." □

Americans elected a clean-shaven Abe Lincoln (below, right) in November 1860, but the president they inaugurated the following March wore the familiar Lincoln beard.

Scalpers

"The hour of bitter distress was the time of his harvest," according to a 19th-century contemporary of Jock Macleod, "and whenever penury knocked at the door, Jock was sure to follow, if there were any fair females within." The stock in trade of Jock Macleod, who prowled the lanes and villages of Devonshire, was human hair, and his best sources were the wives and daughters of families in distress. In good times, their flowing tresses might be the envy of all. In bad times, Jock came calling, and they converted their coiffures into cash. "Often has Jock shorn the locks of a village beauty," wrote his chronicler, that "she has at length sacrificed, with many a smothered sob and bitter tear."

MacLeod was a mere cog in a vast hair-vending machine, however. For several centuries, hair peddlers had been a fixture of the European countryside. These itinerant agents traveled between town and county fairs, where women came to sell their hair. Buying cheap in the countryside, the peddlers would then sell their goods to urban hair merchants, who would retail it to the wigmakers serving the demand of wealthy men and women for fine wigs.

Not just any hair would do. Most highly prized was the snow-white hair of elderly women, believed to retain its bounce and take dye better than any other. Blond and red hair stood next on the list. The best-quality hair, naturally, went into the most expensive wigs; the lowest quality was turned

A French village auction of natural hair in the late 1800s draws a crowd of buyers.

into hairpieces for the theater.

Some buyers took the longer view and cultivated their sources—old women in almshouses especially—returning every two years or so to collect a fresh crop of hair. Others were even less savory. Some ghoulish traders frequented the homes of the recently deceased, searched for combings that could be untangled and sold, or—according to some accounts possibly intended to calm unruly youngsters—stole the curls of children.

The trade was large and lucrative for all but those who sacrificed their hair—they often got nothing or were paid with a kerchief. By the mid-19th century, London was home to three hair merchants, who annually purchased 50 tons of material from Jock Macleod and his ilk. Another 17 businesses were engaged in cleaning, combing, and otherwise preparing hair for the city's 27 wigmakers. At every step, the price of hair was inflated, so that the wigmaker paid 15 to 20 times as much for hair as the peddler paid the women who grew it. But the wigmakers got theirs: A top-quality wig of human hair fetched twice its weight in silver on the London market. Hair was also a major export. In 1859 and 1860, for example, about 100 tons of hair were imported by the United States alone—a figure that had tripled by 1866.

The hair trade soon declined, however. Increasing prosperity in the industrialized nations, a fashion shift toward shorter tresses, and the arrival of synthetic hair-like fibers greatly diminished the buying and selling of hair in Europe and America. Today human-hair merchants have largely moved to the less developed nations of Asia, where modern Jock Macleods ply their trade among the poor. □

Locked in Love

A cameo cherub bearing an arrow to pierce the heart and a torch to ignite the flames of love joins a classical couple decorating the clasp of an 1825 Swiss bracelet fashioned of twisted and braided hair. Like lockets containing the hair of a loved one, such accessories were extravagant gifts intended to bind lovers. But often, such bracelets contained only a token lock from the beloved's head—the rest was woven from hair bought for that purpose from strangers.

Hair Today . . .

Not since the biblical strongman Samson, perhaps, had anyone drawn such power from the possession of abundant hair. New York's fabled Seven Sutherland Sisters' locks—with a total length of more than 36 feet—brought them fame and wealth and a kind of power over the 19th-century American audiences who flocked to see and emulate them.

A product of the day's fascination with the extraordinarily ordinary, the corporate success of siblings Sarah (the eldest), Victoria, Isabella, Grace, Naomi, Dora, and Mary (the youngest) ranks among the oddities of vernacular American history. Reared on a farm in western New York State by an ineffectual Methodist minister, Fletcher Sutherland, and his wife, Mary, the sisters showed an early talent for music. Naomi, in particular, had a noteworthy bass voice. The

girls began singing at church socials and local halls throughout the East and were an instant smash hit—but not entirely for their voices. People were transfixed by their hair. Sarah's locks measured three feet, Victoria's seven feet, Isabella's six feet, Grace's five feet, Naomi's five feet four inches, Dora's four feet, and Mary's six feet.

Their collective career took off when they were hired in 1884 as a sideshow act for the Barnum & Bailey Circus, where, dressed in white robes, the sisters would sing current favorites; but the climax of the act came when they turned in unison to reveal their wonderful hair. The same year they started with Barnum & Bailey, their father created the Seven Sutherland Sisters' Hair Grower. The elixir was concocted from rainwater, witch hazel, bay rum, and other unremarkable ingredients. Whether it worked as advertised or not, the tonic was wildly successful.

After Naomi married J. Henry Bailey, nephew to the cofounder of the "Greatest Show on Earth," he and the sisters expanded the line of hair-care products and oversaw the opening of outlets in New York, Toronto, Chicago, Philadelphia, and Havana, Cuba. Suddenly rich, the Sutherlands built an ostentatious, many-gabled mansion in their Niagara County home, a town now called Cambria. There, they lived with as many as 17 cats, all wearing engraved silver collars, and 8 dogs, and spent their money as quickly as it came in.

Few of the sisters lived to see their empire crumble. Naomi died in 1893 at the age of 35, and by 1924 only three remained: Grace, 70, Dora, 63, and Mary, 60. By then, the long hair that had been their glory had fallen out of fashion, replaced by a post-World War I craze for bobbed locks, which also throttled consumer demand for growth tonics.

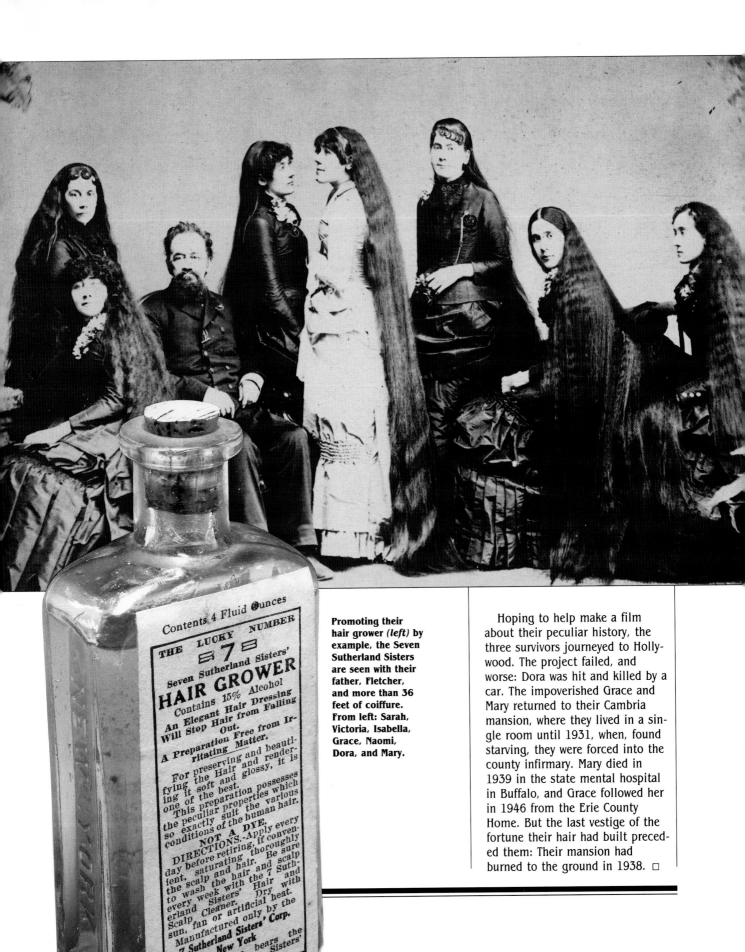

Contents 4 Fluid Ounces

THE LUCKY NUMBER

Seven Sutherland Sisters'

☙ 7 ☙

HAIR GROWER
Contains 15% Alcohol
An Elegant Hair Dressing
Will Stop Hair from Falling
Out.
A Preparation Free from Irritating Matter.

For preserving and beautifying the Hair and rendering it soft and glossy, it is one of the best.

This preparation possesses the peculiar properties which so exactly suit the various conditions of the human hair.

NOT A DYE.

DIRECTIONS.-Apply every day before retiring, if convenient, saturating thoroughly the scalp and hair. Be sure to wash the hair and scalp every week with the 7 Sutherland Sisters' Hair and Scalp Cleaner. Dry with sun, fan or artificial heat.

Manufactured only by the
7 Sutherland Sisters' Corp.
New York

The Genuine bears the Seven Sutherland Sisters' Photograph in group.

Promoting their hair grower (left) by example, the Seven Sutherland Sisters are seen with their father, Fletcher, and more than 36 feet of coiffure. From left: Sarah, Victoria, Isabella, Grace, Naomi, Dora, and Mary.

Hoping to help make a film about their peculiar history, the three survivors journeyed to Hollywood. The project failed, and worse: Dora was hit and killed by a car. The impoverished Grace and Mary returned to their Cambria mansion, where they lived in a single room until 1931, when, found starving, they were forced into the county infirmary. Mary died in 1939 in the state mental hospital in Buffalo, and Grace followed her in 1946 from the Erie County Home. But the last vestige of the fortune their hair had built preceded them: Their mansion had burned to the ground in 1938. □

55

Ondulations

It has been said that a woman possessed of a head of straight hair is a woman in want of a curl. Marcel Grateau staked his career on the wisdom of that maxim and forever changed the look of hair fashion by inventing a technique for producing long-lasting, natural-looking waves in his clients' hair.

Marcel, as he was known professionally, had his defining insight in the 1870s while he was running an unsuccessful hairdressing shop in the artsy, gritty, Montmartre section of Paris. For centuries women and men alike had used heated irons to produce curls in their hair. More often than not, the resulting curl was a transient coil, a tight spiral that quickly degenerated into a frizzy fluff requiring frequent treatment to hold any curvature at all. Experimenting one day with a lock of his mother's hair, which he hoped to restore to its natural undulations, Marcel stumbled upon a solution. With an upside-down twist of the iron and a deft "turn of the wrist," he found that—voilà—he could endow hair with a natural-looking wave. Moreover, the treatment lasted for weeks.

At first, Marcel bestowed the new *moiré* or *ondulation* on his working-class customers gratis. But his policy changed when it became apparent that women were willing to pay for the privilege of having their hair "marcelled," as the process quickly came to be called. Marcel opened a new shop in 1882 near the Théâtre Français and before long counted the great opera divas Calvé and Nellie Melba among his clients. He finally became so much in demand that customers were forced to bid for his services.

In 1897 a wealthy and revered Marcel retired to a château in Normandy at the age of 45, but he did not completely abandon the bright lights of style. Many years later, at a hairdresser's banquet in London, where he was honored for his contributions to the trade, Marcel acknowledged the tribute with characteristic modesty. Recalling his discovery, he said, "I realized at once that I was a benefactor to all womankind." □

In 1922, long after he retired to a Normandy château, Marcel Grateau demonstrates the hair-waving technique that bears his name.

Ruling the Waves

Early permanent waves—touted as "the curl that won't come out"—were administered by a team of technicians who rolled their subjects' hair around chemical-soaked pads and cooked the curls with electric coils for as long as 12 hours in a dangerous-looking tangle of wiring and curlers. This publicity photo shows the first version of a hairdressing machine invented by London hairdresser Karl Nessler—later, Charles Nestlé—in 1904. The Swiss-born inventor later moved to New York, where he transformed his intimidating device into a more compact—and tremendously successful—machine.

Rinse and Die

It must have been one of the more bizarre manslaughter trials ever held in England's Westminster Police Court. In the summer and fall of 1909, hairdresser Beatrice Clark and her supervisor, William Henry Eardley, faced charges that Clark had inadvertently shampooed to death one Helenora Catherine Horn-Elphinstone Dalrymple.

Like some 30,000 English beauty seekers before her, the 29-year-old Dalrymple had come to Harrod's department store, where Clark and Eardley were employed, to indulge in a dry shampoo—a treatment that was supposed to cleanse and rejuvenate the hair, then quickly restore it to dryness. The method involved nothing more than rinsing the hair with a highly volatile fluid, which usually took less than 10 minutes to evaporate.

Soon after Clark applied the liquid, however, Dalrymple paled and said she did not feel well—and then collapsed. Hoping to revive the stricken woman, Clark stretched out her unconscious client on the floor of the cubicle. And there, in only a few minutes, Helenora Dalrymple died.

A postmortem examination found evidence that Dalrymple had suffered from a mild, undiagnosed heart defect—a slight thickening of one valve—as well as a lymphatic condition that might have helped cause her heart to fail. But physicians at the inquest and subsequent trial argued that the real cause was not such minor flaws, but the shampoo. A volatile mixture combining 94 percent carbon tetrachloride, 1.5 percent carbon disulphide, and 4.5 percent scented water, the fluid gave off noxious gases that, experts testified, would

have posed a grave danger to even the healthiest individual. Carbon tetrachloride, they noted, was twice as toxic as chloroform.

Moreover, because the dense vapor from the shampoo was five times heavier than air, it sank down around the head, one reason that shampoo givers seemed relatively unaffected by the fumes. Ironically, Beatrice Clark's well-meaning attempt to make her client more comfortable on the floor had thus increased Dalrymple's exposure to the poisonous gas—and guaranteed her abrupt demise.

The prosecution ultimately withdrew the charges against Clark and Eardley, but the well-publicized medical testimony effectively put an end to the casual use of carbon tetrachloride on human hair. Considered a carcinogen, the substance has been demoted from beauty aid to industrial solvent. □

Needled

There may never have been a time when humans did not decorate their bodies by inoculating the skin with pigments. Archaeologists in Eastern Europe have discovered skin etched with images of fish, birds, and animals on the 2,000-year-old remains of a Scythian warrior, and the ancient Thracians were said to have branded their skin with colored designs. Roman legionnaires posted to Britain learned from Celtic tribesmen the technique of rubbing woad, a blue pigment, into incisions to produce designs that would not wash off. By the fourth century AD, the use of woad on the face had become so common throughout the Roman Empire that upon taking power, Constantine, newly converted to Christianity, banned it as an offense against God. During the Middle Ages the practice was repressed in western Europe, finally reviving in the 1700s, after Britain's Captain Cook returned from the Pacific with a new word: *tattow* or *tatau,* soon Anglicized into tattoo.

Despite its ubiquity, however, the tattoo has been raised to its highest form as an art only in Japan. There, the craft of *irezumi*—literally, "insertion of ink"—is handed down from mentor to disciple and requires remarkable skill.

Among the Ainu, an aboriginal race that once occupied the islands of the Japanese archipelago, the lips, hands, and brows of females were tattooed before marriage. Some historians suspect that when the ethnic Japanese expanded into Ainu territory centuries ago, they picked up the practice, but perhaps not with personal adornment in mind. Instead, they

used the tattoo to brand criminals for life. Some believe that attempts to redraw the brands into something less incriminating led to the creation of ornamental tattoos, especially among the rougher classes. In time it became faddish for prostitutes and working-class men to sport tattoos. Borrowing from the drawings of popular illustrators, irezumi artists called *horishi* began developing a series of standard images and icons based on Japanese myths and legends, a pantheon of threatening deities, folk heroes, carp, and dragons. Such displays went against the totalitarian spirit of the government, which tried to eradicate tattooing along with other forms of individual expression.

The industry persisted, however, drawing clients at first from the ferocious firefighters of Edo—as Tokyo was then called—unemployed toughs hired by the government to combat the fires that perennially raged through the bamboo and paper houses. Adopting neck-to-knee tattoos as a badge of membership in their brigades, the Edo firefighters blazed the tattoo

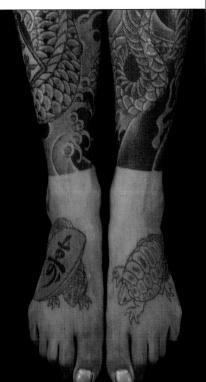

trail. Soon their style spread through the ranks of the so-called naked trades: carpenters, construction workers, rickshaw drivers, and others who worked in loincloths. During the early years of the 19th century, as one historian put it, "the idea of the tattooed man became interesting and attractive."

But not for long. Beginning in about 1830 Japan's government began to change, with the reinstatement of the emperor, a host of reforms, and an opening to Western nations. Loath to be seen as a land of nude, tattooed barbarians, the government dressed the laborers and slapped a ban on irezumi—the term applies both to the art and to the wearer. In fact, visiting Europeans were fascinated by the elaborate tattoos. Irezumi shops, idled by the ban, were allowed to reopen—but only for foreign clients. Among the eager midshipmen to be decorated, legend holds, were England's duke of York, later King George V, and the future czar Nicholas II of Russia.

The techniques of irezumi have changed very little over the centuries. Today, as in ancient times, the master uses an array of penlike implements tipped with needles of varying sizes to tap colored pigments into the skin. Hues include black, which appears as a dark blue under skin, blue, brown, yellow, green, gray, and red. The deeper the pigment's insertion, the richer its color. Unlike the tattooing typical of the West—what one master dubbed "those little things you call tattoos"—Japanese tattoos are subtly shaded, resembling hand-colored woodblock prints. Specialists prefer to execute designs that cover the entire torso, except for the center of the ◊

Tattoo master Horiyoshi III decorated these feet with tortoises, a symbol of longevity.

chest and belly, and extend to the knees and the elbows. The artists achieve additional impact by incorporating movement and contour into the design—body language can transform a dragon, for example, from benign to menacing.

The planning of the enterprise is almost as fraught with ritual as the tattooing itself. Final approval of any plan is the master's, although the client may choose from books showing various designs, and the relationship between irezumi artist and subject is deep and complex.

Since sessions are limited in part by the customer's ability to endure pain, outlining such a pattern may take days, and filling it in with color—the heart of irezumi—can take years. As for full-body treatments, irezumi masters note wryly that such designs are often begun but rarely finished. A work covering almost the entire body, by a certified master, can cost more than $20,000 and take a decade to complete. As with all art, the final touch is the creator's signature on his work.

The resulting "suit" can have the rich detailing of brocade and give the appearance of a second skin, which, in a sense, it is. Because the needles lacerate pores, skin does not perspire from tattooed areas but becomes reptilian and cold. One spouse reportedly complained that going to bed with her fully illustrated husband was like going to bed with a snake.

Tattooing also appears to shorten lives, perhaps because the skin suffocates beneath its covering of choked pores. To a devoted irezumi, however, a shortening of life may be irrelevant. "You never really perfect your life's work anyway," comments one master with a

shrug. "There's always some new place to tattoo, but man dies before his work is finished."

Despite its status as art, irezumi has never quite shaken its rough beginnings. Legal in Japan since the end of World War II, the practice remains largely an underground profession, in part because secretive masters fear their rivals may steal unique inks and patterns or copy innovative needling techniques. Practitioners are not listed in telephone books and foreigners are often told, incorrectly, that such tattooing is no longer done.

More important, perhaps, is the persistent connection between irezumi and criminals. As the tattooing originated in a convict's brand, it has flowered into grand, secret suits covering the bodies of Japanese *yakuza*, a word that means "worthless" but is used with defiant pride by the nation's mobsters to describe themselves. Many gangs flaunt tattoos as a badge of belonging and of manhood.

But irezumi has its forensic, as well as its criminal, side. When Tokyo police turn up a body bearing a tattoo, even a minor one, they call a master, who can immediately identify the hand that made the tattoo. And, for some, this inherently ephemeral art form, designed to last only a lifetime, achieves a kind of immortality. In the pathology department at Tokyo University, researchers studying the health effects of pigmentation have put together a collection of some 100 flayed skins from deceased irezumi. Beautiful yet macabre, hundreds more of these bizarre remains hang as art in restricted galleries, enduring canvases of a strange cosmetic art. □

Wannabe Wodaabes

For most of the year, the 50,000 or so people of the Wodaabe wander across nearly 100,000 square miles of arid central Niger in search of grazing and water for their prized zebu cattle, sheep, goats, and camels. But the Wodaabe take time out to dance, sing, tell stories, celebrate births and marriages, renew acquaintances, form alliances—and stage one of the world's most unusual beauty contests.

Called *geerewol*, the assemblies let groups from different family lines pair off for competitive dances celebrating the qualities that are perhaps most important in the Wodaabe's isolated life: beauty and charm. Each geerewol—to accommodate alliances between the tribe's 15 lineages, many are held—features two grand dances. One is the *yaake*, a contest based on charm and personality; the other, like the gathering itself, is called the *geerewol*. From it, the most beautiful members of each lineage are selected.

Wodaabe men are herders, and when otherwise unoccupied they spend long hours together lounging over tea, discussing the day's events, and carrying on a running, joking, caustic commentary on one another's appearance. The informal competition helps prepare for the competitive rigors of the geerewol fest. Lithe and long limbed, these ancient wanderers have evolved strict criteria of *boodal*, or physical beauty, among them a high forehead, aquiline nose, large eyes, white teeth, light skin, and swan-like neck. But boodal is not ◊

Living canvases, Japanese tattoo master Horikin (near left) and wife wear full suits of deities, demons, flames, and flowers. Her hair hides an unfinished duplicate of the master's tattooed scalp.

The hairline shaved high and eyes accented with kohl, a Wodaabe contestant applies facial makeup to accentuate the aquiline nose and high cheekbones held to be the height of beauty.

Geerewol contestants primp and preen for hours in preparation. They don their finest jewelry and most elaborate headbands and turbans. They wrap their bodies in tight skirts, over which are draped bright, embroidered tunics. To accentuate the whiteness of teeth and eyes, lips and eyelids are blackened with kohl. The skin is lightened with yellow powder, the hairline shaved, and the face artfully decorated with dots and designs to bring out the long noses and bright eyes associated with the Wodaabe ideal of beauty. "We are born beautiful," explains one, "but we also have the power of *maa-gani*—the knowledge of secret potions—to enhance that beauty."

In the yaake, candidates from both clans form a chorus line, and as they approach judges and spectators, the real contest begins: They grin; they purse their lips, roll their eyes, and smile fetchingly to impress the judges with their charm, magnetism, and personality. Old women poke, prod, and heckle them. The three judges—unmarried women chosen from the tribe's most beautiful young females—keep their counsel until the very end.

Togu, or charm, must be enough. It must be accompanied by *togu*, or charm; personal magnetism; and what Westerners would call personality.

The women, who themselves possess a natural elegant beauty, prize the spiritual qualities of *semteende*, meaning reserve and modesty; *hakkilo*, or care and forethought; and *munyal*, patience and fortitude. These qualities are vital to the women's daily work, which comprises the bulk of the nomads' hard labor: The women build temporary shelters in camps, gather firewood, milk cows, tend children, and pound and cook millet.

Teeth flashing in wide smiles, eight statuesque, ornamented Wodaabe vie for the charm championship.

Filigree designs traced in henna paste—the dark compound leaves a reddish stain—adorn the hand of a Moroccan woman.

accompanied by beauty, and to determine the most beautiful there is the nightly geerewol dance. Adorned with strings of beads and headgear decorated with ostrich feathers, the dancers again form a line and begin rhythmically chanting, stamping, weaving, and jumping. As the night continues, the dancing builds in intensity until, after careful modest scrutiny, the judges indicate their favorites.

In most important respects, the yaake and geerewol competitions resemble Western-style beauty pageants. The difference: All the contestants are male. □

Red-handed

Since prehistory, the people of subtropical North Africa and Asia have used the paste derived from the henna bush, *Lawsonia inermis,* to impart an orange hue to cloth and leather. But in Morocco and other strongholds of Islam, henna has become much more than a stain—it is the medium of an exquisite art whose canvas is the feet and hands of women.

From time to time, Muslim women in Morocco break the isolation of their straitened lives with get-togethers called henna parties. A feature of these elaborate affairs, which may last for several days, is the appearance of a craftswoman called a *mu'allima.* In return for cash and gifts of cigarettes and sweets, this artist applies henna paste with fine brushes and modified fountain pens and syringes to trace intricate designs on the hands and feet of the party's hostess. The henna stains the skin, imparting a red-orange hue to the design. Because representational images are forbidden by Islamic doctrine, the patterns are usually geometric abstractions whose swirls and scrolls resemble ornamental ironwork or delicate lace.

The application of henna is an all-day task, concluded by a drying exposure to the heat and smoke of aromatic coals and swathing in protective cloths for the night. In the morning the crusty outer layer of henna is scraped off, and the design is traced once more. The two coats yield an intensely pigmented stain that will last up to a month.

A woman thus adorned wins the admiration of her female neighbors and, wherever she goes, is greeted with the words *B-sahaa-l-henna,* or "Wear the henna in good health." But, according to legend, at least, the rusty patterns have a practical purpose as well. They are intended to attract one or another of the many jinn, spirits who inhabit dark, damp places. If pleased with the design, it is said, a jinn may guard the wearer against ill fortune or grant such blessings as wealth and fertility. □

Lower lip and earlobes enlarged by years of stretching, an adult Mursi woman wears large terracotta plates as a mark of beauty.

The Quality of Mursi

The nomadic Mursi of Ethiopia are among the most assiduously beautiful people on earth. When not making war or gambling, the tribe's lean, six-foot-plus men spend much of their time grooming one another, shaving their bodies completely except for a narrow strip of hair that coils around the crown of their heads.

But it is the Mursi women who are remembered most by all who see them. Each adult wears a plate as large as 10 inches in diameter in her lower lip and smaller plates in each earlobe. In addition, Mursi women raise intricate patterns of coiling snakes and other figures on their bodies by making small incisions in their skin, into which they insert slivers of wood or stone.

Beautification begins at a young age, when a girl's earlobes are pierced and gradually—and permanently—stretched by the insertion of ever-larger wooden disks. At the age of 10, her lower front teeth are removed to prepare for the next step, when, at puberty, her lower lip is slit and a small wooden plug inserted. The plug is replaced by terracotta plates called *pelele*, each larger than the last, because the size of the lip plate is the measure of beauty—and a mark of value to the girl's family. A particularly well-endowed maiden might fetch 40 cows as a bride price.

Ethnologists have speculated about the origins of ear and lip plates. Some believe the disks were devised to identify tribes or to make women unattractive to European slave traders. But all evidence—including the testimony of the Mursi themselves—indicates that the plates were intended simply as arks of beauty. In fact, the plates confer the highest distinction: Mursi women, explained one tribesman, "do not resemble animals." □

Wedding Rings

Of all the modifications of the human body in pursuit of beauty, few are as spectacular as those of the women of the Ndebele tribe of South Africa *(below)*, who lengthen their necks by wrapping them with brass and copper rings until they stretch to dizzying heights.

The rings, called *iindzila,* are donned at marriage; more are added over time until a woman's head may perch a foot above her shoulders. The bands press downward, too, deforming the collarbone. Although the iindzila impose a regal posture and stately gait upon their wearers, they make women's tasks even more burdensome, and many Ndebele women are shedding their traditional ornaments in favor of a less-fettered life.

Some, however, are striking a compromise between tradition and modernity. For example, Nomapitoli Thubana of Kameelrivier shed her iindzila as a practical matter—the rings kept her from "moving fast" on her city job. But she is still part of the tribe, and on special occasions she clips on a set of removable plastic rings. □

Skin Deep

Painfully crafted by rubbing ashes or charcoal into incisions made with thorns, these lines and semicircles of raised scars, or keloids, identify the tribal affiliation of a woman in the Sudan. Scarification is used in cultures throughout the world as tribal marking, initiation ritual, and—frequently—artistic enhancement of the bearer's body.

All the Rage

London designers Diana and Jazz epitomize the avant-garde fashion of the 1990s. Diana's indigo lips and blue-dyed, waist-length hair set off a costume punctuated by silver rope, studs, and rhinestones, which are also worn on her forehead and eyebrows. In contrasting crimson, tattooed Jazz wears an American Indian necklace, a silver death's head pendant, and silver-studded belt and watchband that he designed.

Talent at Her Fingertips

At the age of what she calls "25-and-holding," Liz Fojon of Fair Lawn, New Jersey, arrived at the pinnacle of her profession in 1988. That year, Fojon painted a set of 10, inch-and-a-half-long, portraits of the lanky cartoon character the Pink Panther, dressed in native costumes from as many nations and saying hello in the language of each. Her medium was acrylic water-base paint. Her canvas was a set of artificial fingernails.

The Pink Panthers made Fojon the hands-down winner in the fine nail art division of the World International Nail and Beauty Association's annual championships. The car- ◇

Four hours' effort produced these prize-winning Zodiac-figure fingernails by nail artist Liz Fojon. Her own nails (right) feature abstract designs—and attached gold charms called danglies.

toon characters also helped bring global recognition to illustrated fingernails.

This increasingly popular form of personal adornment may not be for everyone, but for some women—and some men—brandishing scenes of palm trees or the New York City skyline on their fingernails is a fashion statement that cries out to be made. Almost anything goes: Fojon has depicted family portraits, couples making love, storks, teddy bears, Christmas trees, and even pictures of new products for the nails of a photo executive. Sports stars and comic-book heroes are also favorite subjects. Paint is only the beginning of what is possible, however. Fojon will sculpt nails into various shapes, will offer to implant fake diamonds, and will even supply artificial nails draped with chains or charmlike "danglies." Some nails are affixed by fine chains to rings or bracelets.

But Fojon stresses that nail art is about art and not necessarily the size of the fingernails. Outlandishly long artificial nails can pose problems of fungus infections, and very long natural nails occasionally sustain breaks that can tear flesh, draw blood, and cause "like major, total pain," says Fojon. The artist dismisses the notion that long nails must be inconvenient, however, and finds her own two-inch-long talons quite manageable. "If you can't handle your nails," she says dismissively, "then cut them." □

A gold ring decorates the navel of a woman attending a 1991 tattoo convention in Anaheim, California.

Penetrating Insight

As she strode through the midtown Manhattan business world, computer-graphics technician Lauren Hachemeister turned heads with her ring—the one through her nose. But not all of the attention has been favorable. According to a 1991 newspaper report, her distinctive nasal adornment cost Hachemeister her job with a New York law firm. But no matter: The ring in her nose, she says, is an important symbol of her right to "do with my body what I want." Hachemeister maintains that wearing the ring was "part of my pri-

mal calling," an ancient impulse that a growing minority of Americans seem to feel. Body piercing, an ancient art associated with primitive tribes, inexplicably revived in the United States during the 1970s. Now, combining elements of fashionable adornment, physical mutilation, and social rebellion, it has become for many the ornamental rage of the 1990s.

Once the earmark of California's tattoo and leather crowd, the American vogue at first kept to the fringes of social acceptability. But, according to those who have followed—and themselves enjoyed—piercing, new enthusiasts are emerging from the mainstream. Eminently respectable secretaries, doctors, lawyers, and police have begun to skewer conservative convention with secret penetrations of their bodies. ◊

According to piercing aficionados, the man most responsible for single-handedly reviving this aboriginal mode of bodily adornment—at least in the United States—is Jim Ward, the founder of the Gauntlet, a piercing salon that boasts outlets in Los Angeles, San Francisco, and on New York's Fifth Avenue. Ward began his practice in 1975 in the living room of his West Hollywood home, but demand soon outstripped the space and he opened the first Gauntlet store in 1977 on Santa Monica Boulevard in Los Angeles. Since then, his salons have poked about 75,000 piercings—more than 11,000 of them in 1991 alone.

Patrons may choose from a score of "classical" piercings recorded in historical or anthropological texts. There appear to be few pierceable parts that have not been perforated and decorated—navels, nostrils, nipples, ears, cheeks, tongues, eyebrows, and genitals lead the sometimes bizarre list. Usually, piercing is followed by simple adornment; plain rings and tiny barbells made of gold, niobium, or stainless steel predominate, although navel gems and nose bones called tusks are not uncommon.

Unlike routine ear piercing, some of the more complicated adornments run close to minor surgery and, without proper procedures, carry some of the same risks of pain and infection, including such blood-borne disorders as AIDS. Despite the potential hazards, there are many do-it-yourself adherents. For them, Ward publishes a quarterly magazine, *Piercing Fans International,* and offers his video, *Pierce with a Pro,* for sale.

But, to a degree, the bloom is off the rose. While Ward has profited from the expansion of his market, he now laments the loss of serious purpose among some piercees. Once, people got pierced to make a ferocious personal statement. Today, Ward says, young people are just "doing it for shock value, or to be like their peers." □

THE GLASS OF FASHION

Denmark's Prince Hamlet, the melancholy hero of Shakespeare's tragic play, was described by the maiden Ophelia as "the glass of fashion"—the mirror from which fashion takes its cues. What the Bard implied, and what historians regard as axiomatic, is that fashion follows power. But fashion is itself a society-shaping mirror that reveals the trends and tenor of the times in the human parade's ever-changing uniforms. One can read in evolving modes of dress the hand of a powerful queen, the linkage of fashionable folly to moneyed idleness, and traces of a purely practical impulse—for example, the replacement of brilliant battle dress by earth-toned cotton twill.

Often, however, a change in form profoundly alters substance. Whole peer groups have been freed by altered vogues—in their search for equity, women had first to escape from hobbling petticoats; teenagers emerged as a youthful subset of society when they ceased dressing as incomplete adults. Through it all, the aristocracies' lustrous fabrics have been dimmed by the shadows of other figures—men, medieval as well as modern, who dressed in the austere costumes of real potency. Fashion may follow power, but power follows gold.

3

Bursting Forth

In the isolated courts of medieval Europe, the nobility wore almost androgynous ankle-length robes, a costume that had served them well for more than a dozen centuries. But, as life in these enclaves had sedated the impulse toward individual expression, the emergence of towns revived it. The medieval epoch of pious conformity was ending; renaissance was in the air.

Fashion, like war, was then mainly a male province, and men's altered styles may have drawn less from the tailor than from the knight. Armorers had replaced the chain-mail chemise worn by earlier warriors with closely fitted suits of steel, pinched at the waist and as tight as a metal skin. This top-heavy, slender-hipped man in armor soon became the manly paradigm of the day.

Except where age or occasion demanded more conservative attire, long tunics gave way to the shortened, fitted coat and close-fitting hose—a narrow look that some carried to extremes. "In those days the folly of man had gone so far," observed the scandalized *Chronicle* of the City of Mainz describing the late 14th century, "that the young men wore such short skirts that neither their shameful front nor their rear end was covered. If someone had to bend over, one clearly saw his rear. Oh, what an unbelievable shame!" □

These idealized, robed statues of 11th-century Saxon Ekkehard II and his wife, Uta, carved more than a century after their deaths, stand in the cathedral at Naumburg, Germany.

Short tunics swept the post-medieval world. At left, a young man dressed in big shoulders and hip-length tunic *(background)* watches French historian Jean Froissart present his work to England's King Richard II. A 1474 painting of Mantua's Gonzaga family *(top)* by Andrea Mantegna shows young men in tunics but the noble old in robes. A detail *(above)* from the first panel of Vittore Carpaccio's *The Arrival of the English Ambassadors to the King of Brittany*, painted about 1496, depicts even fifth-century diplomats in the stylish costume typical of the Renaissance.

Uncovered by a stylishly short tunic *(left)*, the young man in this 15th-century engraving wears hose that do not quite meet in front. By 1502, when German artist Albrecht Dürer engraved *Standard Bearer (below)*, a triangular flap—called a codpiece in England—had closed the gap.

Band-Aid?

Beneath their buttoned coats, 15th-century men wore a short doublet over a linen shirt tucked into the tops of hose—two separate stockings made from linen or wool. Worn over linen underbritches, the loose hose reached from the foot to the waist, where they were laced to the doublet. But the lacing left a scandalous gap between the two pieces of hose. A cloth gusset was hastily added to cover the posterior, and a removable triangular patch was laced on to connect the segments of hose in the front. In England, this utilitarian flap was called a codpiece.

It was an imperfect solution, to be sure. In 1482, ten years before Italian navigator Christopher Columbus sailed into the unknown, England's King Edward IV asked that a man's coat be long enough to "cover his privy members and buttokkes" and restricted such exposure to the aristocracy. A decade after Columbus's return, however, another kind of codpiece—a large, padded, sometimes decorated pouch—began to appear. Widely viewed today as a laughable flaunting of maleness, the pouches may have had less to do with masculine vanity than with hygiene.

According to Grace W. Vicary, a cultural anthropologist and independent scholar in Cambridge, Massachusetts, the codpiece may have been a specialized bandage for a new affliction.

In 1493 Ruy Diaz de Isla, a physician in the Spanish port of Barcelona, treated some of the first sailors to return from the New World, where they had contracted a deadly contagion never before seen in Europe—one that spread like wildfire through the formerly unexposed population. Known variously as the French sickness, Naples disease, or simply the pox,

the affliction was syphilis.

The primary agents of the epidemic's spread were the French, Spanish, and German mercenaries who marauded across Europe, became infected, and returned home with the disease. According to Vicary, their pouchlike codpieces were improvised dressings to spare the afflicted from jarring contact—and more. Dosed with mercury-laced unguents, men used the codpiece to keep from staining fin-

ery. The codpiece also concealed a condition for which infected soldiers could be sent home. For the aristocracy, it hid a disgracing illness. Then, as the object became high fashion, the issue of disease was mooted—a man could not be judged sick or well just because he wore a codpiece.

Whether the odd device was just sexual nonsense or the strange artifact of a venereal pandemic, it did not last beyond the 16th century. But no one knows whether codpieces fell out of general use or went underground, vanishing into the bloomers worn by the noblemen of Elizabeth's England. □

Among the most flagrant codpiece fashions of the 16th century was the Spanish variant, seen in a posthumous portrait of Don Carlos (above) painted by 17th-century artist Sanchez Coello. But the odd article of apparel, like the vast power of Spain, would soon be gone. An anonymous portrait of Elizabethan poet-warrior Sir Philip Sidney (right) painted in 1577 shows it beginning to disappear between the full-stomached doublet called a peasecod and the broad-hipped lower garment known as melons.

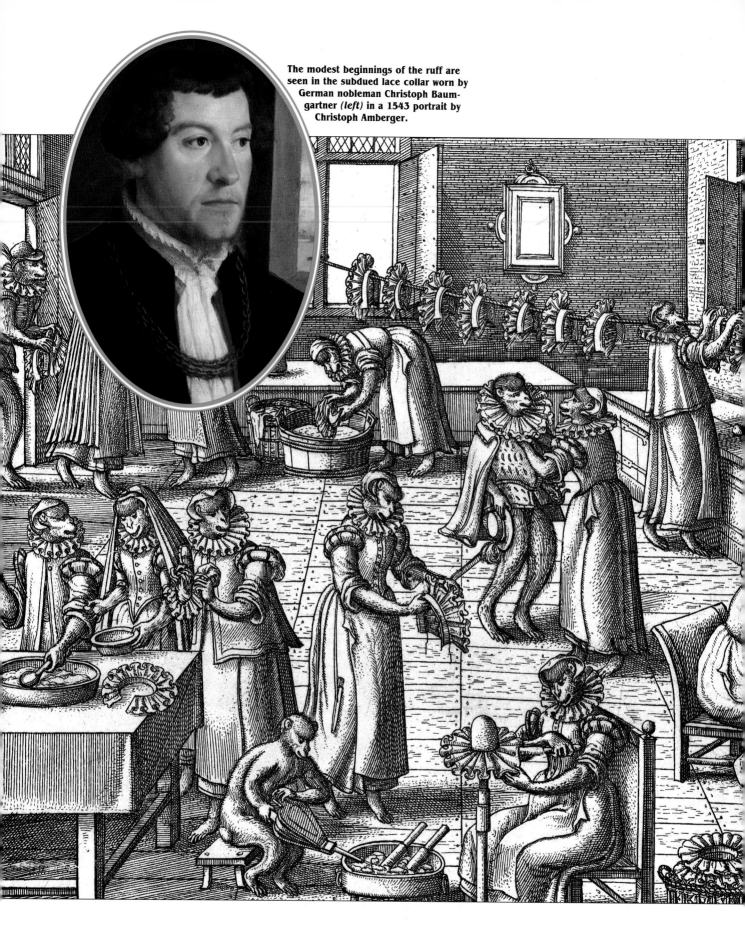

The modest beginnings of the ruff are seen in the subdued lace collar worn by German nobleman Christoph Baumgartner *(left)* in a 1543 portrait by Christoph Amberger.

The Devil's Cartwheel

The ruff—a cumbersome, fragile necklace of starched linen worn by the wealthy—bloomed like a flower on the tree of European fashion for a century, then suddenly wilted. Appearing around 1530 as a modest lace collar gathered by a drawstring, the device swiftly opened into an elaborate construction in which a wire frame was covered with fluted starched linen that was often embroidered with gold and silver needlework and edged with lace. The idea was evidently to display the head as in a portrait, separated from the lower body by a gleaming white field. Whatever the motive that produced it, however, by 1635 the ruff had gone the way of the codpiece, never to return.

While it lasted, the ruff earned a comfortable living for those who laundered and preened these neckpieces of the rich. The launderers extracted starch from wheat or other grains, boiled it into a paste, then slathered it over both sides of the fabric. They molded each accordion-fold flute over a shaped stick and dried the finished product before a fire. Sometimes, heated steel rods were used to shape and dry the ruff simultaneously. The result was fine, but fragile: Ruffs sagged in wet weather.

Fashionable to many, ruffs were anathema to a few. Smelling vanity, English Puritan Philip Stubbes called ruffs "cartwheels of the devil's chariot of pride, leading the direct way to the dungeon of hell"—or to ridicule. "He looks in that deep ruff," observed a character in Ben Jonson's *The Alchemist,* "like a head on a platter." □

The expanding ruff, with hundreds of perfectly starched accordion pleats, appears in the 1632 portrait of Volkera van Bereseijn *(near left)* by Dutch artist Rembrandt van Ryn. At left, *Laundering Ruffs,* an engraving made about 1570 by Crispin van der Passe, depicts the labor-intensive care of ruffs as work for monkeys, shown "apeing the fashion."

Mad Slashers

The mercenary armies that carried war, terror, and disease across 15th-century Europe were also, in their way, purveyors of new styles. The signal design contributed by the landsknechte, as they were called, was a less gruesome kind of slashing.

According to legend, the fashionable mutilation of clothing was invented by the Swiss in 1476, after they defeated the Burgundian forces of Charles the Bold at Morat. The conquest yielded a wealth of velvets, silks, and other finery, which the victors used to patch their own ruined clothing. The resulting colorful patches, applied on the inside of rips in outer garments, became a fad among German mercenaries, who took the custom home with them.

Called slashing, this innovative tailoring perforated doublets, coats, and britches so that the fine material underneath could be pulled out through the slits. Slashing quickly spread to the nobility, who had begun to inflate the ideal male form with padding. The result, like the raised feathers on an owl, was to make the wearer appear larger than life. □

The elaborate clothes-slashing begun by 15th-century European mercenaries (above) was intended to reveal lower layers of rich apparel through slitted outer garments. Slashing reached its high point in Germany, in the extravagantly perforated wardrobes of such splendidly attired nobles as Duke Henry the Pious of Saxony (left), portrayed in a 1514 painting by Lucas Cranach.

Descent of Man

The noblemen of England during the reign of Queen Elizabeth I were men for all seasons, capable of everything from great poetry to piracy and seamanship on the grand scale. But these versatile, courageous subjects of the queen wrapped their qualities in attire that was, compared with the massive glitter of an earlier generation, almost effeminate. Where before men had been padded into giant versions of themselves, the Elizabethans seemed actually to shrink.

Their costumes belied action by binding and shriveling the chests and shoulders in narrow, tight-fitting doublets increasingly embossed with ornamentation. Beneath this seemingly fragile torso, hose-clad legs extended from a padded bell of britches, stuffed to the shape of a plump inverted heart. In the court of their gritty old queen, the contradictions between appearance and performance must have been mere matters of form. No one doubted that a Francis Drake or Philip Sydney, for example, would instantly put down a book of verse to pick up the sword, or that any Elizabethan noble would flinch from his own death.

Without the tough-minded monarch at the center of fashion, however, the distinction between form and substance swiftly faded. During the discredited rule of King James I, men were just what they seemed, and perhaps less. The former court of statesmen and buccaneers, prelates and poets, became one of excess, extravagance, and royal favorites—such frail, contentious parodies of the Elizabethan man as Richard Sackville, of whom a descendant wrote, "His life is an empty record of gambling, cockfighting, tilting." □

Fine-Feathered Friends

On June 7, 1520, beneath fluttering banners and tapestries, two dazzling armies faced each other across the Val d'Or near Calais. On one side, 5,000 English nobles, soldiers, and servants surrounded a glittering Henry VIII, magnificent in a silver gown and a rose velvet doublet, rubies and emeralds flash-

ing on his cap. Francis I of France, a bejeweled satin cloak flung over his own suit of silver cloth, a coif of damask gold sprinkled with diamonds on his head, posed with his elite entourage on the opposite side. At the trumpet fanfare, the two royal peacocks dashed forward and embraced. The spectacle

known thereafter as the Field of Cloth of Gold had officially begun.

Eyewitnesses called the two-week festival of jousting, dancing, and singing—held in the hope of forging an alliance against Spain—the eighth wonder of the world. The Val d'Or had been transformed into a fantastical city of multicolored tents. In the English compound, artisans created a magical four-

story "summer palace" and two wine-spouting fountains. In this setting, the powerful of both kingdoms strutted in costumes of dazzling richness.

Like kings and queens before and after them, Henry and Francis believed that clothing was the ultimate badge of rank. To head off the democratic intrusions of commoners, European rulers passed so-called sumptuary laws, which reserved certain materials, styles, and colors for the upper class. But there was no enforcing such laws—merchants simply wore the proscribed garments and suffered the occasional fine.

In fact, royal fashions had begun to show a hollow center. Long on style but short on substance, such pompous displays as the Field of Cloth of Gold had little real effect beyond the ruination of some attending nobles. As the French ambassador Du Bellay observed afterward, "many carried their mills, their forests, and their meadows on their backs." Some may have felt a chill of waning power, as well, as they played beneath the lengthening shadow of a drab, moneyed, middle class. □

In a contemporary painting of the Field of Cloth of Gold, a gold-robed Henry VIII *(foreground, left)* and 5,000 followers approach the castle at Guines. Surrounded by magnificent tents, the English "summer palace" is seen at right, fronted by a fountain spouting wine.

Henry VIII—portrayed *(right)* about 1537 by the school of Hans Holbein the younger—had little influence on Europe, unlike Francis I of France and Charles I of Spain. Seen in a 1525 portrait by Jean Clouet, Francis I *(above, left)* competed with Spain for the Roman throne but lost to Charles. Though resplendent in a portrait *(above, right)* by Titian, the devout man who became Emperor Charles V of Rome preferred a modest black.

King-makers

During the 16th and 17th centuries, the glittering finery of Europe's great rulers was occluded by a subtle transition: Real power began to pass from majesty to money. The early signs of this important change had come during the competing reigns of two kings—Francis I of France

of emperorship to astronomical levels. The electors scoffed at royal promises of future payment—kings had proved to be disastrously bad risks—demanding cash or something just as negotiable: the promissory note of Jakob Fugger. He gave his word—and a good deal of his fortune—and Charles I of Spain became Emperor Charles V of Rome in 1519.

Charles was so dilatory about repaying his benefactor, however, that, four years later, Europe's most powerful merchant sent the Continent's most powerful ruler a caustic dunning letter. "It is well known," wrote Jakob Fugger, "that Your Imperial Majesty could not have gained the Roman Crown save with mine aid." Had Fugger gone with Francis, he went on, he would have "obtained much money and property, such as was then offered to me."

Still, the Fuggers stayed behind their emperor. When Jakob died in 1526, his mantle passed to his nephew Anton Fugger. It fell to him to save Charles one last time—at terrible cost. In 1552, when the ailing emperor's fate once more rested in Fugger hands, Anton gave Charles a massive infusion of ducats. But not even his dynasty could sustain such support. Their long ties with the rulers of Spain and Rome had triggered a financial hemorrhage in the Fuggers' fortune. The death of Anton in 1560 sealed the great house's fate.

Still, they had set the pattern: From their day onward, the real power behind the stylishly attired kings and queens of Europe would be practical men like Jakob Fugger, who dressed plainly, but held enormous wealth. □

and Charles I of Spain—and a remarkable commoner by the name of Jakob Fugger.

Possessing the crowns of France and Spain, both kings coveted the greater crown of the Holy Roman Empire. Even before failing Roman emperor Maximilian I died in 1519, Francis had begun to bid for the vacant office. But Charles, who had been crowned king of Spain in 1516, had an ace in the hole: He had support from the family Fugger.

An immensely wealthy German dynasty of merchants, the Fuggers had long been associated with the Roman throne. Upon Maximilian's death, the family leader, Jakob, turned to help Charles, the anointed successor. But Francis's interest set off a round of competitive bribing among the German electors that ultimately drove the price

Royal Suit

The civil strife that racked Europe during the early 17th century largely quenched the rich colors worn at court. In England, the extravagant reigns of James I and his indolent second son, Charles, led in 1642 to a bloody revolution that raged until the defeat of the Royalists. King Charles was beheaded by the victors in 1649, and power passed to a quintessential man in black: Oliver Cromwell. Purveyed from pulpits around the land, the fashion message was as unambiguous as the lord protector's wardrobe: plain dress was moral; fancy dress was not.

Seemingly extinguished, however, fashion merely slept. In 1658 Louis XIV, a king who could tolerate nothing plain, took the French throne. Two years later his cousin Charles II regained the crown of England. The royal pair revived a sense of male style, and the body began once again to come out of hiding.

Over the next century, this emerging form was further molded by western Europe's rediscovery of the heroic human form, as preserved in antique Greek and Roman statues. To display their own fine figures, the European men of the 18th century adopted tight breeches the color of pale skin, worn with a short vest, or waistcoat, and open jacket—one of the enduring innovations of Charles II, the three-piece suit. □

A fashion revival produced the so-called Tottering Triangle, seen in the 1663 *Portrait of a Young Man (left),* by Dutch artist Ter Borch. Bulging petticoat britches later forced coattails to be tied back, as illustrated by Dutch engraver Romain de Hooghe's 1664 *Die Mode (above).*

A quintessential man of leg, muslin manufacturer Samuel Oldknow *(left)* wears skin-colored britches in a Joseph Wright painting circa 1790—as does England's corpulent prince of Wales *(below)* in James Gillray's 1793 caricature. Louis P. Boitard's 1737 engraving *(far left)* depicts a young gentleman in a hardy perennial—an early three-piece suit.

Basic Black

Alfred-Guillaume-Gabriel, count d'Orsay, may have led the last great color offensive in the English fashion wars. Arriving in London in the 1820s, the Frenchman dazzled with what one observer described as "the fantastical finery of his dress; sky-blue satin cravat, yards of gold chain, white French gloves, light drab greatcoat, lined with velvet of the same colour, invisible inexpressibles skin-coloured and fitting like a glove." But d'Orsay, like a peacock drowning in a sable sea, soon surrendered to the prevailing style: British black.

Even before the Frenchman's arrival, the pastel, naked-looking leg had fallen out of favor: A society that called pants "inexpressibles" had little room for skin-tight breeches. But the choice of black also had a practical side. In the sooty cities of England's industrial revolution, only the very rich could afford cream-colored garments.

In the unsigned 1832 painting *The Round Pond, Kensington Gardens (above)*, such rural garb as frock coats and riding boots have invaded urban English society, preceding the lounge suit, modeled at left by artist Sir Coutts Lindsay in 1883.

Although adopted by the aristocracy, the black suit was the egalitarian uniform of a growing professional middle class. "The title of Gentleman," wrote one observer in 1840, "is now commonly given to all those that distinguish themselves from the common sort of people by a good suit of clothes." And a very good suit of clothes it was. Judged merely by the cut of their colorless attire, British men were on their way to becoming the best dressed in the world. □

A well-cut power suit, Homburg, and tightly rolled umbrella became a virtual uniform for the British foreign service, as personified by Britain's crisply tailored Sir Samuel Hoare (right), seen strutting his stuff during the 1938 crisis over German territorial claims in Czechoslovakia.

Dressing Down

Few persons living around the beginning of the 19th century could fail to be moved by the spectacle of British troops in uniform. With colorful guidons fluttering from their pikestaffs, the soldiers wore helmets of gleaming steel, rich cloth, and dense fur, trimmed with brass medallions, tassels, streamers, and feathered combs. Long-tailed coats of brilliant red and blue wool were emblazoned with gold braid and flashing brass buckles. The British officers' gleaming swords competed for attention with the brightly polished muskets of the private soldiers.

Here was palpable evidence of military might. There was no distinction between parade dress and battle garb; one outfit served both purposes. The bold colors, flash, and glitter that impressed on parade were in fact as much battlefield weapons as the cannon—an enemy would find such flash intimidating.

The British defeated Napoleon at Waterloo in 1815 and until World War I fought just once more in Europe—in the Crimea from 1854 to 1856. Meanwhile, Britain's soldiers engaged in 80 campaigns in Asia and Africa. There, far from the cool mists of home, the tropical heat and unconventional tactics of native warriors began inexorably to alter soldierly fashion.

At first the changes were informal and irregular. Regimental commanders established their own standards; while many allowed their men to fight in "undress"—light shirts and cloth caps—some stuck by full European uniform. White predominated; camouflage and the need for earthy colors was not yet an issue, as most fighting was at close range. In the beginning, commanders' tastes and the need for comfort in the tropical heat prevailed.

Old ways were not forgotten, however. British soldiers storming Russian lines in the Crimea in 1854 wore the same bright colors and flashing metals they had donned when they defeated Napoleon 39 years before. □

British forces in 1826 *(above)* wore brilliant uniforms for both parade and battle. From left: mounted, 12th Lancers, 1st Dragoon Guards, 10th Hussars, 2nd Life Guards; standing, 2nd Foot, sergeants in the 60th Rifles and 38th Foot (Grenadiers), officers in the 4th Light Dragoons, 93rd Highlanders, 8th Foot (Light Company), 24th Foot (Grenadiers), and 57th Foot.

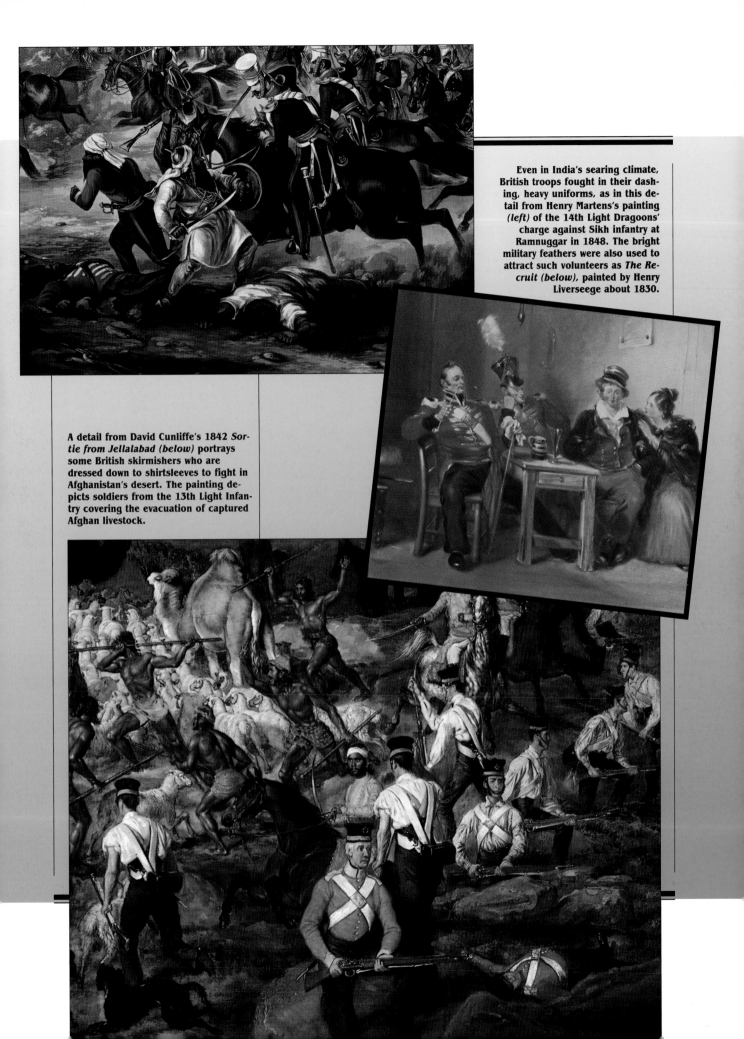

Even in India's searing climate, British troops fought in their dashing, heavy uniforms, as in this detail from Henry Martens's painting *(left)* of the 14th Light Dragoons' charge against Sikh infantry at Ramnuggar in 1848. The bright military feathers were also used to attract such volunteers as *The Recruit (below)*, painted by Henry Liverseege about 1830.

A detail from David Cunliffe's 1842 *Sortie from Jellalabad (below)* portrays some British skirmishers who are dressed down to shirtsleeves to fight in Afghanistan's desert. The painting depicts soldiers from the 13th Light Infantry covering the evacuation of captured Afghan livestock.

The Thin Red Line

In 1854 Britain's army opened its first European campaign in nearly 40 years against Russian troops in the Crimea on the shores of the Black Sea. Among the most resplendent units was the 93rd Highlanders, a regiment whose Scottish pedigree was proclaimed by kilts, brilliant red coats, white boots, and towering bearskin hats.

Victorious once, the 93rd was tested again near the port of Balaclava on October 25, 1854. There, 600 of the regiment's men turned aside a charge of Russian cavalry with a withering barrage of rifle fire. Hours later the assembled cavalry regiments of the Light Brigade began their renowned, but tragic, charge, in which two-thirds of the British horsemen were cut down by Russian guns. While the Light Brigade was mourned and its commanders properly vilified, the Highlanders' brave stand was memorialized in the dramatic, touching name by which they are still remembered—The Thin Red Line.

The instrument of the 93rd's victory, however, had not been color, but a newly issued weapon, the 1851 Pattern Minié rifle. Its 1,000-yard range gave the Highlanders time to loose three volleys on the advancing Russian cavalry; with the old musket the enemy would have been within range only long enough for one volley. The Minié rifle also marked the demise of splendid uniforms worn in the field. The longer range of new rifles meant that soldiers would need to make themselves less visible or be picked off at a distance by enemy fire. □

Robert Gibb's 1881 *Thin Red Line* recreates the 1854 stand of the kilt-clad 93rd Highlanders in the Crimea, where they repulsed an overwhelming Russian cavalry charge. In fact, the Russian horse never got as close as the artist indicated.

Marching on Indian mutineers in Delhi, the 1st European Bengal Fusiliers *(below)* wear undress white shirts and trousers in this 1857 lithograph by Captain George F. Atkinson of the Bengal Engineers.

Dust to Dust

Khaki uniforms—the word *khak* is Persian for "dust"—entered British service and the English language in 1846, when Lieutenant Harry Lumsden outfitted a company of Indian soldiers in loose-fitting clothes dyed a drab gray-brown color so that they would not show soil as easily as white. But British soldiers in India continued to wear their heavy "home" uniforms in battle until the spring of 1857, when native troops, called sepoys, of the British East India Company's Bengal Army revolted at Meerut, near Delhi, and the two-year-long Indian Mutiny began. For the first time, British troops were required to fight in the heat of the Indian summer, which often exceeded 100 degrees Fahrenheit. As a matter of survival, they soon donned make-do, lightweight outfits. Some wore white, but eventually most troops wore clothing dyed to some approximation of khaki.

Earth-toned garb won converts for tactical reasons, too. On India's northwest frontier, where the British fought the Afghans intermittently from 1837 until 1947, red-coated soldiers were easily picked off by Afghan marksmen. Khaki uniforms helped them hide, and by 1880 all British soldiers sent to Afghanistan wore khaki. In contrast, Her Majesty's army, fighting rebel South African farmers in 1881, stuck to red—with disastrous results, as the Boers easily shot down the bright-coated British.

By 1885 the lessons of Africa and Asia had been absorbed, and khaki became the color for all British troops overseas. But the army retained its crimson tunics for the European field. Not until 1902 was khaki officially adopted as the fighting color of every British soldier. □

In Africa traditional red coats were still combat dress in 1879, as seen in *The Battle of Isandhlwana (right)* by Charles E. Fripp. *Last Eleven at Maiwand (above),* painted around 1882 by Frank Feller, shows that British soldiers were wearing khaki into combat on the subcontinent in 1880.

When Lord Horatio Herbert Kitchener counterattacked the followers of the charismatic native leader called the Mahdi, the peer and his men wore khaki. *The Charge of the 21st Lancers at the Battle of Omdurman (above)* is a rendering by Richard Caton Woodville of the 1898 battle that gave Britain victory in the Sudan.

Fiery Hoops

In the hope of achieving "the ample, fan-like form which is so graceful and so rarely obtained," generations of 19th-century European women flared their skirts with whalebone, braided straw, inflatable tubes, and rolls called crinolines—from *crin*, French for "horsehair," and linen. Then, in 1856, an unnamed Frenchman—some historians believe it was R. C. Milliet of Besançon—patented an alternative: a series of spring-steel hoops of increasing diameter that were linked by tape or ribbons.

Dubbed the crinoline, the device permitted women to sit without crushing their ball gowns, imparted a graceful swinging motion, and restored the female ankle to occasional view. Much has been written in retrospect about the hoops' resemblance to a metal cage. But, to those who wore it, the crinoline was a technological breakthrough.

Like most breakthroughs, the crinoline had its problems: The swaying hoops were bothersome to passersby on the street and destructive in a room filled with bric-a-brac. Simply sitting down required space, discretion, and planning. The apparatus was also dangerous. Crinolines sometimes became entangled in the wheels of passing wagons and could upset the wearer in a high wind. Worse, their covering of light fabrics was highly flammable. A horrifying case in point: During a mass for the

An anonymous French caricature *(above)* satirizes crinolined women filling a first-class railroad compartment with their voluminous skirts. At right, an 1862 tableau at a country house photographed by H. W. Verschoyle shows various styles of crinoline, including a slightly shortened design *(second from right)* for croquet and other genteel exercise.

Feast of the Immaculate Conception in 1863, fire swept through a church in Santiago, Chile, killing some 1,800 women trapped there by panic and their immobilizing, incendiary crinolines.

"Take what precautions we may against fire," warned London's *Illustrated News of the World* in 1863, "so long as the hoop is worn, life is never safe." By the 1870s the crinoline craze was on the wane, but not because of fire—it was time for the bustle. □

A skirt is gingerly lowered to cover a metal-hoop crinoline petticoat *(right)* **nearly six feet in diameter in this 1860s image by French photographer Sirot.**

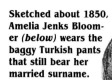

Bloomer Bust

One of the first shots fired in women's fight for emancipation was not aimed at the issues of equality or the vote, but at the oppressively stuffed floor-length fashions of Victorian times. In 1849, in her newsletter, the *Lily*, 31-year-old Amelia Jenks Bloomer proposed a shocking, but eminently practical, new kind of attire for women.

Bloomer described the costume, which had been designed by her friend Elizabeth Smith Miller, as a walking dress of "changeable figured silk, purple and white, extending two or three inches below the knee." Its most controversial element was a pair of baggy Turkish trousers worn beneath the shin-length skirt and cinched at the ankle—a garment since called bloomers. Although conservative by modern standards, bloomers were quickly condemned as indecent; worse, critics accused bloomered females of stealing male styles. But the press liked both the garment and its attractive young proponent and spread Amelia Bloomer's name across the Western world. In England a cheerful song about the costume, "I Want to Be a Bloomer," soon made the rounds.

But not many women of the time really did want to be bloomers or to confront the harsh criticism and merciless ridicule that greeted wearers. "Woman has always sacrificed her comfort to fashions," exhorted Amelia Bloomer in the *Lily*. "Fit yourselves for a higher sphere and cease grovelling in the dirt. Let there be no stain of earth upon your soul or apparel."

Despite such moving harangues, the Bloomer costume remained the dress of only a few nonconformist women who were bold enough to wear it at the lectern and on the streets. Indeed, when Dr. Mary Walker, a physician who had served in the American Civil War, donned trousers and a skirt in New York in 1866, she attracted so much attention that a policeman was forced

to detain her at his precinct. "Had the Bloomer costume," wrote one observer in 1854, "been introduced by a tall and graceful scion of the aristocracy, instead of being at first adopted by the middle ranks, it might have met with better success."

Instead, Victorian women embraced another passing fancy, the metal crinoline (pages 94-95). But bloomers were by no means finished. They merely needed a reason for being—the bicycle, as it turned out. □

In 1885 female tourists crossing the Mer de Glace in the French Alps *(above)* still wear long skirts and bustles, ignoring the exhortations of such proponents of rational dress as the viscountess Florence Harberton *(right)*. Photographed in about 1890, she wears the bifurcated costume that once caused her ejection from a Surrey hotel.

Peddling Knickers

When British inventor H. J. Lawson unveiled his variant of the bicycle in 1876, he helped ignite a global cycling craze—and also struck a blow for 19th-century women. Unlike its large-wheeled predecessors, Lawson's machine, a forerunner of modern bikes called the Safety, was light and easy to handle. For the first time, the freedom of the open road became accessible to exercise-minded women. But liberation also posed an ageless question: What to wear?

Cycling in ordinary daywear was difficult even with the frame lowered. Mounting and dismounting in ankle-length dresses was awkward and embarrassing, as it sometimes exposed hidden limbs to public view, and voluminous skirts were easily entangled in the spokes and the chain. Many female cyclists around the world yearned for what they called rational dress—bloomers and knickers. But others were more cautious, fearing that wearing such costumes was tantamount to impersonating men.

The ensuing dilemma was neatly illustrated in Christchurch, New Zealand, where the Atalanta Cycling Club—one of the first women's cycling organizations—was founded in 1892. Some members held that the club uniform should follow convention, not comfort; others urged rational dress. The debate raged for weeks in the local newspaper.

In New Zealand—as elsewhere—the matter was finally mooted by compromise. The Atalanta Cycling Club decided not to decide. Members would wear a cap and tunic on top; the lower half was a member's choice. □

During the bicycling craze that swept the world in the late 19th century, many women found it hard to mount and ride the machines while wearing a full-length skirt *(left)*. Others solved the problem *(right)* by adopting a split skirt—despite glares from respectable passersby of the carriage class. Members of the Atalanta Cycling Club *(above)* of Christchurch, New Zealand, were themselves split in 1892 over whether their cycling uniform skirts should be full or divided.

Terns for the Worst

During the second half of the 19th century, millinery took a strange ornithological turn. The bizarre fad grew out of the period's fascination with nature and the commercialization of taxidermy, which had formerly been a collector's art form. Decorations that had begun as a single feather in the 1860s— foot-long white egret plumes were a favorite—evolved by 1890 into hats bearing an entire stuffed bird, couched in a setting of leaves, twigs, and moss.

A highly profitable plumage trade sprang up in London, then spread to North America, where abundant bird populations seemed to offer unlimited supplies of decorative feathers. But the slaughter was unprecedented: Hunters who made their living killing birds sacrificed 5 million to fashion each year; one gunner boasted of bagging 4,000 gulls in a single season. The ensuing avian carnage quickly pushed some species to the brink of extinction. When the graceful white egrets of the American south nearly disappeared, the hunters simply moved north to shoot terns and gulls. With the fad for feathers raging, most people ignored charges of cruelty and calls for wildlife preservation.

But a few citizens were sufficiently concerned to band together against what they called "the demands of a barbarous fashion in millinery." In 1896 a group of proper Bostonians founded the Massachusetts Audubon Society, the ancestor of today's Audubon societies, and its members organized other groups, hired game war-

Corseted into an imposing pigeon shape, an unnamed New York woman (*left*) wears a stuffed bird on her hat in this 1901 photograph by Louis Alman.

dens to enforce existing laws, and applied their influence in Washington and state capitals.

Audubon historians attribute some of their eventual success to warden Guy Bradley. In July 1905, patrolling the mangrove-covered coast of southern Florida, Bradley had come upon the schooner of local plume poacher Walter Smith and had seen Smith's son come aboard with four dead egrets. ''I want to arrest your son,'' Bradley told Smith, who watched him over the barrel of a repeating rifle. When the warden approached, Smith shot him in the chest. Two boys found Bradley's body the next day. Smith was not indicted for the crime, but the murder touched a nerve across the United States. A similar murder of warden Columbus G. MacLeod in 1908 stiffened public outrage. By 1913 state and federal laws outlawing the plume trade were in place; in 1916 a treaty with Canada stopped the North American trade in birds. The British Parliament finally followed with its ban in 1921—after the sober styles of World War I had driven the plumage business to extinction. □

Attending the Eton-Harrow cricket match at Lord's in 1900, young Etonians *(right)* wear a cutaway version of adult attire.

Mountain of Youth

For proof that fashion follows power as unerringly now as it did in the days of Henry VIII, historians point to a uniquely modern case: the invention of the teenager. Until the middle of the 20th century, these writers note, the young were regarded as merely unfinished adults. Children dressed as small adults who sprouted into full-size ones, and teeners, as they were sometimes called in Victorian England, aped their adult counterparts, not one another. After the explosive birthrates of World War II, however, the seamless evolution from child into adult acquired a kind of intermission in which the young waited for maturity.

As with so much in Western society, one of the early signals of this younger world order was felt on the fashion front, with the appearance in the early 1950s of Britain's Teddy Boys. These fashion plates imitated the turn-of-the-century Edwardian styles favored by the postwar upper classes. Soon, in a neat reversal of an ageless custom, young working-class people were creating fashions of their own design.

Youth quickly lost its taste for the costumes of adulthood. Suits became the contemptible, conservative uniforms of the grown and were discarded in favor of casual dress and sec-

ondhand clothes picked up in charities. Rampant in Britain and Western Europe, the trend was strongest in the United States. There "it is definitely the age of the crazy-mixed-up kid," observed British playwright Noel Coward.

"The whole nation seems to be becoming increasingly juvenile."

But the conservation of youth by youngsters was only one face of the teenage coin. The obverse was the desperate pursuit of youth by the aging. Instead of boys and girls aspiring to be men and women, men and women tried to retrieve their adolescence by donning youthful disguises. □

As a separate teenage culture evolved, 1950s jitterbugs *(opposite)* gave way to a 1960s breed *(right)* that favored long hair, beads, and denim.

$neaker$

When 15-year-old Michael Thomas of Anne Arundel County, Maryland, shelled out $115.50 for a pair of black leather basketball shoes endorsed by superstar Michael Jordan of the Chicago Bulls, he made the most important purchase of his young life. "Before I let anyone take those shoes," he told his grandmother, "they'll have to kill me." Two weeks later, someone did. On May 2, 1989, Michael's barefoot body was found in the woods near his school, and a 17-year-old basketball-playing chum was charged with strangling the youngster and stealing his Jordans.

Owning a pair of sneakers was not always a life-and-death matter. The first shoe featuring a rubber sole and canvas upper—the basic elements of all such footwear—was called a croquet sandal when it appeared in 1868. The new design was snapped up by rich Victorians who needed something comfortable for playing croquet and tennis. But the working classes were not drawn to a pricey six-dollar shoe that had been named for an upper-crust lawn game.

By 1873, however, the same sandals had been recast as sneakers—a term that probably refers to the silent tread of a soft rubber sole. In 1897 Sears and Roebuck offered their sneaker at about one-tenth the original price: 60 cents.

Over the years, despite such refinements as arch supports and ventilating eyelets, the sneaker remained a cheap, humble, canvas-

Putting comfort ahead of chic, model Merry Grusenmeyer *(above)* carries her heels and wears her running shoes on New York's Fifth Avenue during a 1980 transit strike. In the same practical spirit, actress Cybill Shepherd *(left)* flaunts the athletic footwear she picked for the 1985 Emmy television awards.

and-rubber creation used mainly for sports. Several generations called them tennis shoes.

During the fitness-conscious 1970s and 1980s, however, these peripheral articles of clothing moved to center stage. Manufacturers introduced the running shoe, made on a slightly curved last that gave the shoe more flexibility as the foot rolled forward from heel to toe. Soon there were shoes tailored to every sport, from squash to cycling, made of suede and nylon as well as canvas and rubber. As a final stylish touch, the new shoes were splashed with iridescent accents. The sneaker had become the athletic shoe.

But the new footwear connected to sports in ways that had more to do with fantasy than fitness. The athletic shoe conveyed upon the wearer some of the revered athlete's aura—an illusion fed by advertising. Partly because of this, sneakers have become potent symbols of status and power in America's inner cities, where there is little of either. Urban teenagers may be judged solely by the style and price of their athletic shoes. "The fact is," explains one youth, "you *are* what you wear—on your feet." Hundred-dollar sneakers are part of a gang's exclusive uniform, or "colors"—intruders are beaten for wearing the wrong brand of athletic shoes onto another brand's turf.

Curiously, the shoes have acquired their strange power at a time when the generation that created them has turned back to simple canvas-and-rubber footwear—the tennis shoes of childhood. But in the cities, the modern sneaker remains the shoe for young men to kill, and die, for. □

Seen in 1988, New York's Julio Colon (left), then 17, reportedly spent half his weekly salary to build a collection of some 50 pairs of high-priced sneakers.

Poly Gone

Polyester, a man-made fiber that is incapable of being wrinkled, soiled, or creased, has come to signal its wearer's station and taste, much as ermine once denoted royalty. But the artificial thread points just the other way. Polyester today has become a pejorative synonym for synthetic.

Developed by British researchers during World War II, polyester entered modern life in 1963, when an Illinois chemist named Delbert Meyer discovered a better way of producing the material. Then, as now, the new threads were blended with natural fibers to create clothing that felt almost like cotton or wool but was washable and wrinkle resistant. But the era's quintessential garment—the leisure suit—was pure poly.

Cut from rolls of spongy double-knitted polyester, leisure suits ran to earth tones, blues, racing green, maroon, and the entire spectrum of pastel hues. Airless and incredibly warm in hot, humid weather, polyester leisure suits clung to their wearer's arms and legs no matter what the season. The highly flammable synthetic melted when it burned and stuck to its wearer like napalm.

Upper-class men were not impressed with the laborsaving innovation and stayed with their real cottons, silks, and wools. Leisure suits were just too democratic—as one fashion writer put it, they made everybody look like a bus driver. But many liked the design. "I loved them," laments Van Harden, a midwestern talk-show host. "They were functional, you didn't need a tie, and food slid right off"—unlike ermine. □

Wearing his polyester best, radio programmer Dave Campbell strikes a disco pose with wife Annette during 1992's Fourth Annual Leisure Suit Convention, which drew 1,200 enthusiasts to Des Moines's Val Aire Ballroom.

TRENDSETTERS

The pace of fashion in every age has been set by the deft, often powerful, touch of men and women who, by virtue of place, personality, or some special resonance with the spirit of the time, are widely emulated. Monarchs have always driven fashion before them—the stylistic dictates of a potent king or queen once had the force of meteor strikes, and even modern royals have exerted great influence on prevailing notions of what is fashionable.

But a new breed of royalty has entered the field since Elizabethan times, an aristocracy of money, fame, power, talent, and, often, sheer exposure. Presidents and politicians, actors, musicians, designers, athletes—the vivid presences who sense and articulate some hidden yearning of the multitudes—are scrutinized for style cues. In fact, many of these high-profile figures are in the business of finding and feeding such needs. Still, no one follows a single paradigm. The day when the sky of fashion can hold only a single shooting star—an Elizabeth, a Brummell, a Chanel, or a Pompadour—has passed. Today, legions of trendsetters clamor for attention, their myriad offerings less like the blazing passage of a heavenly body than the shards of brilliance in a kaleidoscope—intermittent, shattered, and ephemeral.

Fit for a Queen

As the child of Ann Boleyn, the abandoned—and beheaded—second wife of King Henry VIII, the young princess Elizabeth lived in virtual exile within the royal household and in penury. "She hath neither gown," complained the royal governess in a plea for funds, "nor petticoat, nor no manner of linnen." But two decades later, when the little princess succeeded to the throne of England, she put those gownless times firmly behind her. From the beginning, her reign was an epoch of glittering raiment, still a legend today.

For her coronation procession in January 1559, Elizabeth I rode in an open litter draped in gold brocade and was herself resplendent in gilt cloth trimmed with ermine. "The court so sparkled with jewels and gold collars that they cleared the air, though it snowed a little," a foreign emissary wrote. Having raised a gilded curtain on a reign that would last 44 years, Elizabeth began to introduce some of the most extravagant fashion the world has seen. Hers was an age that loved display, and no one fed and guided that appetite more than the queen. So huge was her wardrobe that it inspired one of the lesser-known Elizabethan innovations: the closet as a special room, with a separate hook for each dress.

Elizabeth's nobles curried favor with gifts of clothes and jewels—she created a vogue for multiple ropes of pearls—and eagerly aped her example, sometimes bankrupting themselves. When a cleric dared to criticize her vanity and profligacy, she told her ladies hu-morously that if he persisted she would "fit him for heaven—but he would walk thither without a staff and leave his mantle behind him."

Vain though the queen was, her display was not motivated solely by vanity. Clothes also signaled royal strength. To her subjects and rivals, domestic and foreign, Elizabeth was the embodiment of England in all its glory; she dressed as she wanted England to be seen. Clothing was also a badge of class and position; by law, the queen alone might wear purple, and only nobles could wear gold trim.

Portraits of Elizabeth show a woman imprisoned by starched ruffs and the immense boned underskirts called farthingales. Her clothes were richly embroidered, often with symbolic figures: roses for her Tudor lineage, lilies for her chastity. Colors had symbolic value, too, and toward the end of her reign the Virgin Queen—and her loyal courtiers—wore mainly pure white, symbolizing chastity, humility, and faith. Other colors bore names that evoked both the poetry and the earthiness of the Elizabethan age: popinjay blue, mulberry, pease porridge, lustie-gallant red, goose-turd green, puke brown, dead Spaniard beige. There was even *couleur Isabelle,* a dirty ecru named for the presumed color of the Spanish queen's petticoats, which Isabella had sworn not to change until the Moors were driven from her realm.

The English ruler's ladies-in-waiting followed their mistress, but only to a point, for no

As she grew older, Elizabeth grew more immoderate and ever more anxious about seeming to weaken with age. Accordingly, the queen enameled herself with white-lead makeup—reputed to be almost half an inch thick in some places—and painted faint blue veins over the pale pancake to mimic the translucent skin of youth. She covered her thinning hair with bright red wigs. The rest of the court followed, as usual. Mirrors, which Elizabeth's reign had brought into vogue, were banned from the royal presence for her last 20 years.

Elizabeth died in 1603 at the age of 69, wearily dragging her rail-thin figure around in the same outsize dress day after day or lying on piles of pillows to prop up her heavy farthingale. The Virgin Queen left a careful inventory of nearly 2,000 items of clothing and jewelry—a legacy that Anne of Denmark, King James's queen, could not ignore, despite her vow never to wear hand-me-downs. Soon after James I took the throne, the Italian ambassador reported that "court dressmakers are at work altering these old robes for nothing new could surpass them." □

one was allowed to outshine the queen. On one occasion Lady Mary Howard, an attendant, made the mistake of wearing an exquisite velvet dress laden with pearls and gold. Elizabeth tried it on, and all agreed it was too short. "Why then," Elizabeth icily told the lady, "if it become not me as being too short, I am minded it shall never become thee, as being too fine: so it fitteth neither well."

The queen modulated what men wore, too. The masculine bulk of Henry VIII gave way to an effeminate silhouette, shaped by tight corsets, boned and padded hose, leg-of-mutton sleeves padded for plumpness, high heels, and a curious garment called the peasecod belly that made men look a bit pregnant *(page 75)*. Not to be left behind by the ladies, who went to great lengths to dye their hair to match the queen's, noblemen tinted their beards auburn or gold.

Draped with ropes of pearls, Queen Elizabeth I *(left)* stood for painter Marcus Gheeraerts the Younger about 1592 in a bejeweled gown of silk and silver with great false sleeves and a winglike veil. A stomacher squeezes the royal waist above a full, flounced skirt supported by a frame of bone and wire hoops called a farthingale. Above, surrounded by musicians and courtiers, the Virgin Queen dances the volta with her favorite, Robert Dudley, earl of Leicester.

Golden Rule

French king Louis XV gave her the title marquise de Pompadour; for nearly 20 years she was his closest adviser and confidante and, for a time, his official mistress, or *maîtresse en titre*. The designation was too modest, for Pompadour, not Louis's wife, Marie Leszcynska, was the de facto queen of France, influencing the course of both its politics and culture. She had not come to such power accidentally but had skillfully stalked and captured both king and country.

Born Jeanne-Antoinette Poisson, the daughter of a Parisian bourgeois, the woman who would become Pompadour was a young matron, Madame d'Etioles, when she set her beribboned cap for Louis. Part of her strategy was to follow the king's hunt through the forest, one day wearing a light-blue dress and in a rose-colored phaeton, the next day in a blue phaeton and a rose-colored dress. Inevitably Madame d'Etioles caught Louis's eye, and he became determined to know her better. At a court ball, she dressed—appropriately, given the circumstances—as the huntress-goddess Diana. The king disguised himself and his courtiers as eight yew trees. Soon there were only seven yews in the ballroom; courtiers glimpsed the eighth tree departing with Diana. Louis—and France—had discovered Pompadour.

Portraits of La Pompadour reveal no great beauty to modern eyes; her nose is beakish, her chin weak. But her charm, intelligence, and forceful personality soon laid claim to Versailles. Before long, to be fashionable was to be *à la Pompadour*. In the morning, chic women wore *déshabille à la Pompadour*, a seductive robe with a tight jacket and flowing skirt. They copied the look of the dresses she designed for herself, confections of ribbons and bows, flowers and lace, and heavy, ornate fabrics incorporating pink and blue bouquets.

In grooming, too, Pompadour kept the court on its bejeweled toes. "A hundred entrancing ways did she arrange her hair—now powdered, now in all its own silken glory, now brushed straight back, ears showing, now in curls on her neck," gushed a 1754 issue of *Connoisseur* magazine, "till the court nearly went mad attempting to imitate her inimitable coiffures." Imitating her fragance must have been maddening, too; Pompadour spent a half-million francs annually on scents. She purportedly bathed in crushed wild strawberries, after which she was massaged with sponges of fine silk saturated with violet-scented milk.

She brought the age's great artists, actors, philosophers, and musicians to Louis's court, but her heart lay in the decorative arts. The mid-18th century was the golden age of rococo ornamentation, an elaborate and fantastical style of which Pompadour, whose instincts for interior decoration may have exceeded even her talent as a royal companion, was the greatest patron. So overwhelmingly elaborate was the ornamentation of the rococo period that it cried out for an equally boldly rendered architecture to accommodate it. The king and his mistress happily complied, embarking on a building and remodeling spree that resulted in some of the finest houses in France. Pompadour crammed each with furniture, paintings, statues, drapery, linen, and silver, all wrought by the finest craftsmen and artists of the age. She hired the painter François Boucher to decorate the rooms. Perhaps her most enduring accomplishment was the establishment of the porcelain factory at Sèvres to compete with Germany's artisans at Meissen and supply Versailles with china and bibelots.

Maintaining a position of leadership in the arts, amusing Louis, and advising him in affairs of state left Pompadour little time for rest. Never a healthy woman, she had to struggle harder each year to put on her best face. Although the king loved her to the end, Pompadour had long since yielded her place as his mistress when she died in 1764, aged only 42. Ever the courtesan, she reportedly insisted on being rouged while on her deathbed, possibly to hide a ghastly pallor. But she told her attendants not to change her clothes. It tired her, said the marquise de Pompadour, and it was no longer worthwhile. □

Beau's Art

In Regency England, a time that may have seen the high-water mark of foppishness, George "Beau" Brummell was the arbiter of style, setting its rules and enforcing them with an iron hand—exquisitely gloved. He brought to men's fashion a dark, well-tailored elegance that has been the enduring standard—as one historian writes, his influence over men's wear "continues so long as evening wear is black"—and he was so devoted to his sartorial calling that his name is still a synonym for dandy.

Born George Byron Brummell in 1778, son of the private secretary to Prime Minister Lord North, Beau used family connections, innate charm, and taste to maneuver himself into lofty circles. The dandy's flair for fashion had become apparent while he was a schoolboy at Eton, where he had distinguished himself by the way he wore his collar

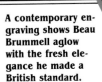

A contemporary engraving shows Beau Brummell aglow with the fresh elegance he made a British standard.

and cravat. After a three-year stint in the 10th Light Dragoons, the prince of Wales's regiment, the 19-year-old Brummell began his career as a man of fashion, supported by a £2,000 annuity from his father. While serving in the 10th Dragoons, he had caught the eye of Britain's top fop, George Augustus Frederick, the prince of Wales, whom the bold young man began to make over in his own impeccable image.

The prince, like most of his contemporaries, was inclined to equate ruffles and doodads with elegance. Personal hygiene was less important than fashion. Brummell brought cleanliness and a novel simplicity into vogue; following his model, dandies wore their hair cropped and unpowdered, shaved their beards, and paid closer attention to their linen. A man emulating Beau Brummell changed his clothes at least four times a day. Brummell's own daily toilette was nearly a theatrical production. Among other rituals, he scrubbed in a milk bath and plucked his eyebrows and whiskers using a dentist's mirror and tweezers, before finally putting on his clothes. Friends would come to watch the spectacle of Brummell getting dressed. Eschewing ruffles and ornamentation, Brummell demanded that his clothes have perfect fit. To that end, he ◊

In an anonymous sketch, Beau Brummell *(left foreground)* chats with the duchess of Rutland at an 1815 ball at the stylish London haunt of Almacks, as guests wearing the fashions that Brummell inspired look on.

claimed, he had the thumbs of his gloves cut by one firm, the fingers by another. He invented stirrup pants, which remained unwrinkled because they were held down by straps that passed under the foot's arch. They were worn with tasseled Hessian boots, which Brummell burnished with champagne. He also gave his contemporaries the thoroughly starched cravat. The fashion of the day called for men to wear a cloth around their necks, and most obeyed with a sagging and often grubby neckerchief. Brummell wore a square of snowy muslin so starched that it had the effect of an orthopedic brace. He spent hours wrapping it around his neck to obtain the perfect trio or pair of wrinkles. As he worked, his rejects fell to the floor. "Our failures!" Brummell's valet grandly told a visitor perplexed by the piles of crushed muslin.

Brummell took the rumpled country look that had just become the fashion in town and gave it a sleek, spare, well-starched style. In his hands, the colors of a former era dissolved in British Black *(pages 86-87).* Where Beau led, well-dressed Englishmen followed, and even the prince, whose corpulence did not lend itself to elegance of line, was persuaded to abandon his gaudiest foppery in favor of fine tailoring of rich fabrics.

Never one to pull his critical punches, Brummell was given to such utterances as, to a distinguished earl, "Bedford, do you call this thing a coat?" Not even his royal patron was spared the sharp Brummell tongue. A contemporary wrote that the prince once "began to blubber when told that Brummell did not like the cut of his coat." Another encounter at a party was simply offensive; Beau re-

portedly turned to the prince's companion and asked, "Who's your fat friend?" The story may be apocryphal—Brummell was rarely so coarse. But his friendship with the volatile prince of Wales—who in 1811 became prince regent, ruling England on behalf of his insane father, George III—soon ended. By about 1816, the arbiter of taste had fallen from royal favor and from public view. At 38, Beau Brummell was a has-been.

But worse was yet to come. Brummell was overtaken by the inexorable arithmetic of his own extravagance. Running with noblemen with incomes many times his own, he had exhausted his resources and gone deeply into debt. To escape his creditors, Brummell fled to France, where he lived in sordid poverty and died in an asylum, dressed in rags soiled by incontinence, in 1840. □

Fashionworks

"The men believe in the Bourse, and the women in Worth," wrote an observer in Paris during the latter half of the 19th century. He might have added that Worth was probably less subject to caprice than Paris's volatile stock market. For 35 years a former English shop assistant named Charles Frederick Worth designed clothing for virtually every famous woman in Europe, defined *chic* for the most fashionable city on earth, and transformed an industry of "little dressmakers"—almost exclusively female—into the global business of high fashion, or haute couture.

Little in Worth's family background foreshadowed such success. The Worths were a family of solicitors in the provincial English town of Bourne. His father, William, lost all his money—whether to drink, gambling, or bad investments is not known—and deserted his family, leaving his youngest son, Charles Frederick, to be apprenticed at the age of 12 to a London dealer in fine fabrics. Young Worth discovered that he possessed a talent for the trade, and in 1845 the enterprising 20-year-old set off for Paris with little money and less French—but immense ambition.

After two years of menial jobs, Worth found a position with Gagelin, Paris's most exclusive fabric house, married one of its models, Marie Vernet, and six years later, in 1857, opened his own dressmaking house. Marie became Worth's greatest clotheshorse—and his best salesperson. She strode the streets of Paris wearing her husband's superb creations and called on the city's great ladies, winning the patronage of such women as Pauline von Metternich, wife of Austria's ambassador to France, who proved instrumental in furthering Worth's ambitions. When the princess Metternich arrived at a royal ball wearing a gown of white tulle spangled with silver and pinned with diamonds, Empress Eugenie of France demanded the name of the Austrian's dressmaker. Her query instantly assured Charles Worth's reputation and laid the foundation of a dynasty.

Worth's trade was built on a reputation for superb fit and the finest workmanship. His gowns, reflecting his clients' tastes, were lavishly detailed, with pearl tassels, silk fringe, feathers, lace, rosettes, and braid. With Princess Metternich's help, Worth repeatedly assaulted accepted styles. He discarded the bonnet in favor of the hat, replaced the shawl with wisps of taffeta and lace, and raised hemlines to clear the ground.

The Englishman's costumes for the French court's frequent masquerade balls were fantasies in fabric. Women sent their precious gems to the House of Worth on the day of a ball to be stitched into the evening's gown. He dressed Princess Metternich as a milkmaid, yoked with solid-silver pails; as Night, in dark-blue tulle covered with diamond stars; as the devil, with two little diamond horns. The empress Eugenie was served up as the wife of the doge of Venice, in black velvet ◊

Mrs. Cornelius Vanderbilt, wearing a costume designed by Charles Frederick Worth, masquerades as Electric Light for the March 1883 Vanderbilt ball.

Worth, in his own estimation, no longer made dresses—he composed toilettes. He was an artist who wished to be compared with the likes of Rembrandt; indeed, Worth gave up mere gentleman's dress in favor of such artistic touches as a velvet beret, a flowing coat edged with fur, and a floppy silk scarf. Worth's ego became the match of his overwrought creations. "The 1870 Revolution," he once commented, referring to the rebellion that deposed Napoleon III and replaced the monarchy with France's Third Republic, "is not much in comparison with *my* revolution: I dethroned the crinoline!"

Before he died in 1895, Worth had enthroned a dynasty. Both of his sons, two grandsons, and two great-grandsons became couturiers. By some accounts the House of Worth was the first high-fashion establishment to introduce lines of maternity clothes and sportswear. And Worth established the customs that came to rule the entire business of fashion: the presentation of the spring and autumn collections, the use of live models, the creation of exclusive designs, and the selling of toiles, or fabrics, and paper patterns.

Somehow, Worth overlooked one product: perfume. This remarkable omission was rectified by his sons in 1900, filling out the line. Ironically, only one wing of the vast House of Worth survived World War II: the latecomer, called Parfums Worth, is still sold today. □

caught up by diamond brooches to reveal a scarlet satin underskirt. For other luminaries, there were angels with wings of swans' feathers; mermaids in watery green and blue tulle set with silver scales; and, time and again, peacocks, with trains decorated with the bird's fabulous plumes.

Worth became a wealthy man, living in a sprawling château and so highly regarded that he could select his clients from among the great. He was the couturier of choice for nearly all the European courts. Wealthy Americans made pilgrimages to the House of Worth. Theatrical stars flocked to him. For fit, fashion, and elegant innovation, there was nothing to compare with Worth's creations. Even Worth's simplest day costume cost 1,600 francs—enough to dress a respectable woman in the city of Paris for a year.

By the 1860s Charles Frederick

The First Edwardian

"He takes no interest in anything but clothes, and again clothes," complained Albert, prince consort to England's Queen Victoria, of their eldest son. Albert Edward, prince of Wales, was just too frivolous. "Even when out shooting," his father went on, "he is more occupied with his trousers than with the game!" The prince was barely 17 when this conversation took place, but already he was exhibiting the traits that would distress his sober-minded parents —and stamp his name upon a glorious, if ephemeral, age.

As prince of Wales, Albert Edward—Bertie to the royal family— began his reign over the world of fashion some 40 years before ascending to the British throne in 1901. He rewrote its rules to accommodate his whims and what were known as his "pleasant little wickednesses": Bertie liked his women and racehorses fast, his food rich, his cigars thick, and his clothing exemplary. The prince's dash and verve supplied welcome relief from stern Victorian restraints. The impeccably tailored and barbered Edward, prince of Wales, set the manly look in England and abroad. He owned a roomful of uniforms and possessed a commanding knowledge of how and when each should be worn. He was a stickler for sartorial perfection, noting with horror the gaffe committed by a guest wearing the wrong buttons, waistcoat, or military ribbons. Edward employed a squad of valets; two traveled with him to help him change clothes as often as six times a day, while the

rest stayed home to tend to his vast wardrobe. Bertie's collection of hats alone topped 100.

Edward's detractors called him "a tailor's dummy," but neither he nor his many admirers cared. New clothing stores opened in London to meet the demand created by a heightened male consciousness of dress. Following Edward's lead, men doffed their hard-blocked bowlers and their Panama hats and donned the soft Homburg. They adopted casually belted Norfolk jackets and tan gloves with black stitching and creased their trousers along the sides rather than the front. Even Edward's stylistic mishaps were copied. The prince's appetite was big, and so was his girth. When Edward left his bottom waistcoat button undone to accommodate his growing stomach, even slender men followed

suit. In one of his many efforts to lose weight, he took up lawn tennis; so did society. An injured elbow led him to shake hands with his arm pressed tight against his side; fashionable men imitated the "Prince of Wales handshake."

The prince laid down the rules, too, for marital behavior or, more precisely, misbehavior. According to the mores of the time, Edward and other upper-class gentlemen could freely conduct affairs with women of lower social position—and did so. But liaisons between Victorian gentlemen and ladies of equal social status were considered unacceptable until Bertie undertook a series of very public affairs with prominent ladies, including a famous relationship with Lillie Langtry *(pages 116-117)*.

Following his example, others bedded society matrons with impunity—and got away with it so long as they maintained appearances. ◊

Edward, prince of Wales *(above, center)*, **created a host of styles for men, including the Homburg hats he and some friends are wearing. His wife, Princess Alexandra** *(left)*, **popularized fringed bangs and a "dog-collar" necklace.**

At weekend house parties, adulterous couples were put into nearby but not adjoining bedrooms, with name cards in small brass holders on the doors to prevent embarrassing mistakes. A gentleman paying a tea-time visit left his hat, gloves, and cane not in the hall but in the drawing room, to give the impression that he had merely dropped in for a few minutes.

Having set the style for roaming men, the prince, perhaps inadvertently, influenced the dress of women. Because the elaborate clothes of the time discouraged quick flings, ladies began slipping into tea gowns that were loose, lacy, and, best of all, worn without corsets. By the turn of the century, women of fashion—and even of virtue—kept a handful of such "teagies" in their closets.

Bertie's tolerant wife, Princess Alexandra of Denmark, also steered women's fashions. No mean dresser herself, she popularized the "dog-collar" necklace, a band of pearls or black velvet fastened by a brooch, that she adopted to cover a tracheotomy scar. Women took up the "Alexandra," a fringe of curls across the forehead.

King Edward VII succeeded his mother to the throne in 1901, when he was 60, and occupied it until his death in 1910. As king, Bertie managed to combine regal dignity with an unabated zest for living, carrying out his largely ceremonial role without relaxing his firm but gentle grip on the empire of fashion. But his memory today evokes much more than style and high living. During the interval now called Edwardian, Britain enjoyed a prosperous bonhomie that, by 1915, had dissolved forever in the horrors of World War I. □

Jersey Lily

They were known as "professional beauties," and in an age when photography was new and the appreciation of feminine beauty was strong, their pictures were as eagerly collected as baseball cards are today. Of all the professional beauties to adorn England in the late 19th century, none was thought lovelier—nor was more widely followed—than Lillie Langtry, the acknowledged mistress of England's Edward VII when he was prince of Wales *(pages 114-116)*.

Lillie Langtry was born Emilie Charlotte Le Breton in Jersey, one of Britain's Channel Islands that lie close to France. With her voluptuous figure, Grecian profile, violet eyes, and petal-white skin, she quickly captivated London's artistic set when she arrived there in 1875, the wife of wealthy Edward Langtry. Oscar Wilde gushed such poetic

tributes as "Lily of love, pure and inviolate!" and brought her amaryllis. John Everett Millais painted her in black, holding a lily, and called the portrait *A Jersey Lily.* By the time the painting was shown at the Royal Academy in 1878, Lillie was the particular friend of the rakish prince of Wales, a style setter and crowd pleaser in his own right. The portrait had to be kept behind ropes to protect it from throngs curious to see the prince's consort. American painter James McNeill Whistler helped decorate the couple's love nest.

Traditionally, English society had looked to its royalty to set fashions. Queen Victoria, however, mourning Albert in her widow's weeds, was an uninspiring model. But as Edward's mistress, the beautiful and spirited Mrs. Langtry—by now estranged from her husband—more than sufficed, and she became one of the first celebrities to create a distinctive look.

Women copied the Langtry hairstyle, featuring bangs and a loose knot at the nape. They flocked to milliners to buy the Langtry hat, a simple toque she had made from black velvet and a quill. They demanded copies of her shoes, her parasols, her cloaks and muffs, and the shade of pink of the dress she wore to the horse races at Ascot. She even created a vogue for the jersey, the knitted garment that, until then, had been worn mostly by fishermen back home. Where Lillie went, people followed. Ladies in ballrooms stood on chairs to study her. People ran after her in the street. A young girl who strongly resembled her was so heavily mobbed that she passed out and was taken to the hospital.

But Lillie Langtry's hold on Bertie had begun to weaken. Although he remained a friend and admirer throughout his life, the prince's royal passion for the Jersey Lily ebbed within a few years, and Lillie had taken a new lover, a friend, aide, and distant cousin of Edward's, Prince Louis of Battenberg. This liaison, which produced a daughter, Jeanne-Marie, also proved temporary. In 1881, finding herself with a baby and no means of support, the resourceful beauty went on the stage.

Critics thought Langtry's early theatrical performances were not quite up to her previous real-life roles. But her audiences loved her and—no doubt helped in part by Edward's faithful presence at her opening nights—she acquired a huge following in her new career. After sweeping England, she formed her own company and headed for the United States on the first of many tours. She traveled the length and breadth of North America in a private railway car built for her by Freddie Gebhard, a Baltimore businessman who became one of her lovers. Another devotee was

rough-cut "Judge" Roy Bean, the justice of the peace, bartender, and promoter also known as the Law West of the Pecos, who changed the name of his Texas town from Vinegarroon to Langtry.

In 1882 Lillie became one of the first women to endorse a commercial product, collecting £132 from the Pears Soap Company; the fee was chosen, she said, because it matched her weight. On one of her American visits, she obtained a New York apartment in exchange for endorsing a line of cosmetics.

Eventually settling down in England, Langtry continued to prosper in a variety of business ventures. Her estranged husband—consigned to the shadows for more than 20 years—died in 1897. Two years later the woman who had consorted with great artists and princes became a lady by marrying the son of a baronet, Hugo de Bathe, on her home island of Jersey. She died in 1929 at age 75 in her villa at Monte Carlo. □

Although Pear's boasted a physician's approval, it was Lillie Langtry's name and image that sold the soap.

All-American Woman

As America approached the end of the 19th century, a captivating creature enchanted the nation and set a new standard of beauty. She was the Gibson Girl, named for New York illustrator Charles Dana Gibson, who brought her into the world in 1890, in the now-vanished weekly satirical magazine *Life*.

Until that time, the United States had slavishly followed European trends in form and fashion. Before the Gibson Girl appeared, the Victorian ideal of womanhood reigned—buxom, bustled, stately, and as unapproachable as the British queen for whom the era was named. The Gibson Girl went just the other way. She was wholly, splendidly, American—tall, sweet, graceful, athletic, and even regal in her amiable way. Her skirt swept the ground, but with less bulk than that of her Victorian sister. Gibson's girl's collar stretched her neck and scratched her chin, but beneath it her shirt front was pleated and comfortable. Her waist was trim, sometimes wasplike, certain evidence of an active, healthy life. In a word, Gibson's creation was the superior product of an energetic, optimistic nation.

Almost immediately, the Gibson Girl was ubiquitous. She could be seen on the golf links, on the tennis court, and in the salon. By 1894 she had become a national sensation. Admired by men, she was also loved by feminists and social reformers, who saw the perfect image of the "new woman."

The press adored her. "As soon as the world saw Gibson's ideal it bowed down in adoration, say- ◊

ing, 'Lo, at last the typical American girl,'" crowed the *New York World.* The *World*'s hyperbole was matched by a European commentator, who gushed: "Parents in the United States are no better than elsewhere, but their daughters! Divinely tall, brows like Juno, lovely heads poised on throats Aphrodite might envy."

Young women of all classes labored to become Gibson Girl lookalikes. They donned girdles, pushed up their bosoms, stretched their necks, grew masses of upswept dark hair, wished for pert noses, and drew rosebud mouths with lipstick. But despite all manner of mechanical aids, few had the natural attributes required; short, stout, or otherwise ordinary females could hardly compete. The phenomenon surprised Gibson. The illustrator had innocently modeled his creation on his beauti-

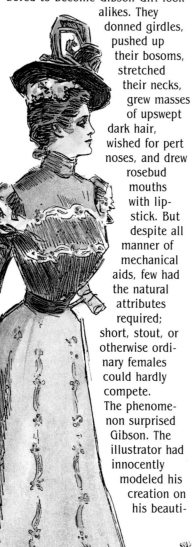

ful, sophisticated sister, Josephine Gibson Knowlton. "If I hadn't seen it in the papers," he once said, "I should never have known that there was such a thing as a Gibson girl." But Gibson also had an artist's appetite for sudden success. He spun out nine illustrated albums that became coffee-table standards. He licensed images for reproduction on spoons, wallpaper, umbrella stands, pillowcases, and any other object capable of bearing his princess's dimpled likeness.

There was, of course, a wide gap between the image and reality. No doubt more than one would-be Gibson Girl found tennis was difficult to play in a long skirt or wondered how one could swing a golf club while cinched by the girdle. There was no point even considering riding a bicycle, the fad sport of the day, in the Gibson uniform—the artist thought the bloomers worn by women cyclists unbecoming. Like her life, the Gibson Girl's social circle was far different from that of most of her imitators. In Charles Dana Gibson's drawings, his creation moved in the same refined circles of society that he enjoyed. She was never found at work, teaching school, or studying at college, as were many women of her generation.

Nevertheless, according to Josephine Gibson Knowlton, the artist's sister, her brother had planted the seed of change. "The Gibson Girl," she once said, "carved a new kind of femininity suggestive of emancipation." Although replaced after World War I by the boyish flapper figure of the 1920s, the Gibson Girl had raised female expectations—and, in her deft, effortless way, set the stage for future generations of unfettered women. □

There Was a Little Girl . . .

With her blond corkscrew curls and invincible innocence, movie star Mary Pickford captured America's heart in 1910 and held it for nearly two decades. Her star rose as America embarked on World War I —soldiers reportedly entered combat wearing lockets containing her miniature portrait—and remained ascendant as the nation struggled to come to terms with a world permanently changed. America and the world needed a sweetheart, and little Mary fit the bill.

Hers was a Cinderella story of sorts; for Pickford, theater became the magical glass slipper. Born Gladys Smith in Toronto in 1892, the girl was thrust into the theater in 1898, at age six. Her father had died, and her mother was desperately seeking a way to support herself and three children: Gladys, Lottie, and John. A fellow boarder at their rooming house was the stage manager at a Toronto theater, and he suggested the bright, blonde, little Gladys and her siblings might find a role or two.

By 1901 Gladys and the others were established fixtures of Toronto theater, thanks largely to their mother's shrewd management. Soon they were touring Canada and the United States and in the off-season living with another stage family whose daughter would also be a movie star, Lillian Gish. Their 1906-1907 season—and the team—ended in Brooklyn. When the rest of the Smiths returned to Toronto, 14-year-old Gladys, by then an eight-year theatrical veteran, stayed in New York.

The young actress's strategy was

simple: She would meet Broadway producer David Belasco and become great. She accomplished both, along the way becoming Mary Pickford, a surname that she borrowed from her maternal great-grandmother. In 1909 Pickford met pioneer movie director D. W. Griffith, who introduced her to the medium that would make her fa-mous. Not everyone shared the director's enthusiasm for films, however. "I suppose we'll have to say goodbye to little Mary Pick-ford," said playwright William de Mille. "She'll never be heard from again, and I feel terribly sorry for her." Despite her own misgivings about leaving the stage, Pickford—along with her manager-mother—followed the movies to Hollywood.

Although she had never really had a childhood by reason of her early career, girlishness was Pickford's stock in trade; her mother and the studios conspired to keep her in curls forever. In Hollywood, they supplemented Mary's own trademark ringlets with hair bought from Los Angeles pros- ◊

Amid oversize props, 27-year-old Mary Pickford *(left)* plays the 10-year-old title role in the 1920 film *Pollyanna.* Eight years later, Pickford publicly shed her child's curls *(above),* a handful of which *(inset)* are preserved in the Los Angeles Museum of Natural History.

titutes, dressed her in organdy pinafores, and furnished her sets with oversize tables and chairs to make her appear juvenile. So successful were these devices that, in 1920, at 27, Pickford played a 10-year-old Pollyanna. Even offscreen, her behavior was so demure that, when Mary finally wore lipstick, good girls knew they could too.

Good and bad, girls everywhere strove to emulate little Mary Pickford. Her ringlets were copied throughout America—even by other actresses. Grown women adopted her demurely girlish dresses, many originally designed for her by couturière Jeanne Lanvin.

Eventually, however, Pickford tired of the little-girl image. On June 21, 1928, after first alerting the press, she left her husband, swashbuckling star Douglas Fairbanks, in their suite at New York's Sherry-Netherland Hotel and marched into a 57th Street salon. There, under the gaze of reporters, she ordered the nervous proprietor, Charles Bock, to clip off her corkscrew curls. Newspapers around the world published photos of the freshly shorn actress. The event, they proclaimed, marked the end of innocence.

The truth was that America had already outgrown "little Mary." Naughty Clara Bow and other flappers had eclipsed Pickford's girlish charm; within a few years her screen career was over. But she had worked hard—harder than most of her contemporaries—and built a fortune as a cofounder of the United Artists film studio with Fairbanks, director D. W. Griffith, and comedian Charlie Chaplin. When she died in 1979, at the age of 87, the little girl with the curl was worth $50 million. □

Losing It

According to writer Elinor Glyn, the quality called It was "an inner magic, an animal magnetism," as well as her novel's title. Clara Bow *(below),* Hollywood's first sex symbol, had so much of It that, for a few high-flying years in the 1920s, women everywhere tried to look like her, mimicking her trademark pencil-thin eyebrows, bee-stung, cupid's-bow lips, yearning saucer eyes, and short, tousled hair.

Bow was born in Brooklyn in 1905, the daughter of a ne'er-do-well waiter and a mother given to mental breakdowns. Her father abandoned the family intermittently; her mother tried to kill Clara on more than one occasion. Bow was just 16 when her vampish good looks helped her escape. A fan-magazine contest gained her a bit part in a movie. Filmed in New York, her scene ended up on the cutting-room floor; but Bow stayed in the business and eventually landed a series of roles in Hollywood produc-

tions. Although most of the films were undistinguished, her performances stood out.

Then, in 1927, *It* struck. Adapted for the screen by Elinor Glyn from her popular flapper tale of a seductive shopgirl, *It* turned Clara Bow into the hottest "jazz baby" of the Jazz Age. She was the quintessential flapper, wrote F. Scott Fitzgerald, who defined the species as "young things with a splendid talent for living." But Bow's talent for living may have exceeded her talent for film. The It Girl lived the part offscreen as well as on, and her name was soon linked to a series of scandals involving drugs, adultery, bribery, and blackmail. Worse, with America heading into the Depression of the 1930s, flappers were losing their following, and Bow's fans fell away. The advent of talking pictures finished her career, for Clara Bow stammered and had never outgrown a Brooklyn accent so thick that it seemed almost self-parody.

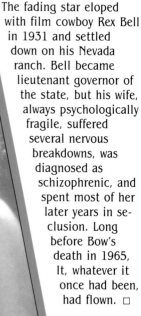

The fading star eloped with film cowboy Rex Bell in 1931 and settled down on his Nevada ranch. Bell became lieutenant governor of the state, but his wife, always psychologically fragile, suffered several nervous breakdowns, was diagnosed as schizophrenic, and spent most of her later years in seclusion. Long before Bow's death in 1965, It, whatever it once had been, had flown. □

Madam C. J. Walker *(below)* made millions on hair-care products sold by hundreds of "agents," seen at right during a 1920s gathering at Walker's Hudson Valley mansion, Lewaro.

Hair Care

When she died in 1919 at Villa Lewaro, the luxurious Hudson Valley mansion for which the great Italian tenor Enrico Caruso had coined a name, Madam C. J. Walker was one of the wealthiest women in the United States and the first to become a millionaire in business. Yet when Caruso and other distinguished visitors came calling, they often rubbed shoulders with African-American hairdressers as well as wealthy whites, this in a

day when blacks were all but invisible to white society and commonly abused. Born Sarah Breedlove, and herself the daughter of former slaves, Madam Walker was widely known and respected among members of all races. Well aware of her unique position, she used it to lobby energetically on behalf of the less fortunate.

Improbably, Madam Walker had built her fortune not on oil wells, steel mills, or railroads, the great capital ventures of her day, but on hair care. She devised a hair treatment and line of products that were marketed door-to-door throughout North America and the Caribbean. According to her own account, a dream had freed her from an inordinately hard life. Orphaned at age 7, married at 14, and left a widow at 20 with a 2-year-old daughter, Sarah Breedlove McWilliams had toiled for 17 years as a St. Louis washerwoman, during which time she married and divorced her second husband, who drank heavily. She also began to lose her hair, not an uncommon occurrence among people who suffered from poor nutrition and bad health care, and where a punishing twist was used to straighten hair.

Then in 1905, Walker recounted later, she prayed for help. The answer had come to her in a dream: a formula that would one day be known as Wonderful Hair Grower.

Later that year, with her hair and her morale rejuvenated, Mc-Williams took her life savings of $1.50—a week's pay—and moved to Denver to make a fresh start by selling her product to other black women. Soon she married newspaperman Charles J. Walker and with his assistance began aggressively marketing the hair grower and two other hair products designed specifically for black women: Glossine, meant to add luster, and a substance called Vegetable Shampoo. Adding a touch of glamor and dignity to the enterprise, she adopted the name Madam C. J. Walker. Unlike competitors, who usually used models with decidedly Caucasian features, Walker put her own distinctly African-American image in advertisements and on labels.

Propelled by Madam Walker's shrewd business judgment and selling talents, the business took off like a rocket. For decades, across the United States and the Caribbean, thousands of neatly dressed saleswomen sold her ◊

products door to door and set up beauty salons in their homes, where they administered the Walker System of hair treatment. In this, a client's hair was shampooed, dressed with Wonderful Hair Grower, and pressed with hot metal combs specially designed by Walker to accommodate her customers' normally thick, tightly curled hair.

The shrewd businesswoman faced more than the usual commercial perils—her products compelled her to cope with a difficult social dilemma as well. At the turn of the 20th century, as now, hair straightening was seen by many black Americans—whose natural hair texture may range from thick kinks and tight curls to loose waves—as a humiliating surrender to white notions of beauty. Yet few black women then wore the hair styles of their African ancestors, and many in some way sought to emulate the feminine ideal promoted in the mass-market magazines of the time—the wasp waist, full bosom, and long, upswept hair of the Gibson Girl *(pages 117-118)*. Companies vied to sell them products that would help manipulate their hair. Some, such as the product Kinkilla, frankly promoted hair straightening. Others disavowed that goal; NOT A HAIR STRAIGHTENER, shouted one advertisement.

Madam Walker ignored the hair-straightening debate when she could, insisting that her process and products simply made hair care and a healthy scalp more easily attainable. Forced to confront the issue, however, she responded with ecumenical zeal. "Right here let me correct the erroneous impression held by some that I claim to straighten the hair," she once told a reporter. "I want the great

masses of my people to take a greater pride in their personal appearance and to give their hair proper attention." All she was selling, she said, was good grooming.

But Madam Walker was also selling hope. Her goals transcended the trivia of waved hair or cosmetic beauty. "To be beautiful does not refer alone to the arrangement of the hair, the perfection of the complexion or to the beauty of the form," she wrote. "To be beautiful, one must combine these qualities with a beautiful mind and soul; a beautiful character." She created the Walker College of Hair Culture to provide a character-building alternative to menial labor for black women. Its graduates were her saleswomen, whom she called agents; they could earn from two to five times the average black domestic worker's wage. She also contributed many thousands of dollars to colleges and benevolent organizations, built homes for workers in Indianapolis, where she located her factory for a time, and created a system of prizes to reward agents who did philanthropic work. Already a contributor to the National Association for the Advancement of Colored People, Madam Walker became an outspoken supporter of efforts to pass a federal antilynching law and do away with the myriad Jim Crow laws governing where, when, and how black people might appear and behave in the American south.

By the end of Walker's short, hard-fought life, business had clearly taken second place to political activism and philanthropy. In 1919, as the 51-year-old millionairess lay dying of kidney failure, she murmured her last words: "I want to live to help my race." □

Radical Chic

In 1926 *Vogue* magazine carried a sketch of an elegantly attenuated woman wearing a dress that was stunning in its simplicity: a black crêpe de Chine sheath with long, close-fitting sleeves and a knee-high skirt. A creation of Paris couturière Coco Chanel, the dress, *Vogue* predicted, would become "a sort of uniform for all women of taste." To those who doubted that stylish women would be willing to forfeit the uniqueness of haute couture, the magazine countered that no one would decide not to buy a car because it was identical to thousands of others; similarity was a guarantee of quality. "Here is a Ford, signed 'Chanel,' " *Vogue* declared. In fact, Chanel's "little black dress" proved more enduring than Ford's monochrome Model T.

At the time, women were still squeezed into corsets and bedecked in furbelows. When Chanel introduced her new fashion, they eagerly embraced the elegant comfort of the new look. Men, at first, were more critical. "No more bosom, no more stomach, no more rump," grumbled some male critics, who dubbed it the "lop off everything" look. But where women led, the fashion industry had to follow. In the decades since, other designers have tampered endlessly with the dress—subtracting sleeves, dropping necklines, and raising hems—but the design remains eternally Chanel's.

Simplicity and comfort were the hallmark of Gabrielle Chanel. Born out of wedlock in 1882 in rural France and orphaned when only 6, she grew up poor and, at 21, began working as a tailor's assistant in Moulins, where she was courted

A 1926 *Vogue* sketch *(left)* launched Coco Chanel's elegantly simple, but enduring, "little black dress."

by French cavalry officers. It was there, one night, that she took the stage of a nightspot called La Rotonde to sing a popular lament about a dog named Coco, lost at the Trocadero. Coco became her nickname and her trademark.

Chanel finally escaped poverty and Moulins by becoming a cocotte, as the pert and pretty companions of wealthy men were called. Her ambition lay elsewhere, however, and eventually, in 1913, Arthur "Boy" Capel, a goodhearted Englishman who had made a fortune in coal, helped her buy a boutique in the fashionable seaside resort of Deauville and encouraged her budding talent. His death in a 1919 auto crash desolated Chanel, who called him the one real love of her life.

Despite her grief, Chanel was finding her course in fashion. From the start, she was determined to "rid women of their frills from head to toe. Each frill discarded," she said, "makes one look younger." Ironically, some credit for Chanel's little black dress could be claimed by a rival couturier, Paul Poiret. By Chanel's account, she decided on her design when, at an opera gala, she was repelled by the sight of hordes of women in the gaudy colors of Poiret's New Dawn. "This can't go on," she declared. "I'm going to stick them all into black dresses." And so she did.

Poiret sneered that her simple designs were "poverty de luxe." Women, he asserted after *Vogue* published Chanel's 1926 creation, were once "architectural, like the prows of ships." Now thanks to Chanel, he mourned, they resembled "little undernourished telegraph clerks."

But Chanel

was also in the right place at precisely the right time. In Paris in the mid-1920s, black had become a wildly fashionable metaphor for a new simplicity and naturalness, as personified by an American jazz dancer by the name of Josephine Baker. Just a year before Chanel introduced her little black dress, Josephine Baker had appeared wearing a G-string made of bananas and little else and had captivated Europe. *La vogue nègre* had swept over the French fashion world. Decorators and jewelers, poster makers and silversmiths all "went Negro," in the phrase of ◊

In 1957, after a 10-year hiatus in Switzerland, Coco Chanel *(above, at left)* was back in Paris, refining her simple line with such touches as these modeled variations on the Chanel look.

the time. Department-store mannequins were lacquered black. Arriving on the scene in 1926, Chanel had added black to her calculatedly narrow spectrum of beige and neutral colors and captured that same natural purity of spirit.

The designer's innovations proved remarkably durable. Her 1926 entries also showed women wearing relaxed raincoats with useful pockets; two years later she introduced featherlight tweeds and twin sets of sweaters trimmed with crisp white collars. In 1930 Chanel brought costume jewelry and the simple jersey to high fashion. She added bell-bottom slacks, leather belts, crocheted lace, small hats, and short evening dresses to women's wear, along with a subtle fragrance simply tagged with her lucky number: Chanel No. 5.

In effect, Chanel helped create a new woman—and helped make the cocotte obsolete. But she herself never quite reformed. A cohort of lovers marched beside the parade of fashions, some of them trouble. After World War II ended in 1945, for example, Chanel was vilified by her compatriots for an affair with a German officer during the occupation. Stung, Chanel retired for nearly a decade to self-imposed exile in Switzerland.

Then, in the 1950s, the septuagenarian couturière reappeared on the Paris fashion scene, introducing the enduring garment now known simply as the Chanel suit—a trim, tailored outfit with a braided cardigan jacket. Once again, Coco Chanel was news, the vivid companion of the famous, and even the subject of a 1969 musical, *Coco*. Not even her death in 1971, at 89, quite released her hold on women's dress. □

Prince of Ties

Britain's Edward VIII proved to be a feckless monarch, abdicating his throne in 1936 after 325 days to marry American divorcée Wallis Warfield Simpson. But in matters of style, Edward was more durable. As prince of Wales in the 1920s and early 1930s, he set the pace for fashion-conscious men everywhere—and left a legacy for men's wear greater even than that of Beau Brummell's *(pages 111-112)*.

While Edward had the benefit of a boyish figure and the best tailors in London, what made him a model for other men was, by one contemporary account, his "marvelous blend of propriety and nonchalance." Disdaining the stiff formality of the royal family—"We had a buttoned-up childhood in every sense of the word," Edward once recalled—he freely experimented with his wardrobe in ways that were frequently garish, sometimes appalling, but always eye-catching.

The prince redesigned some clothes and put others together in unlikely combinations, mixing checks with stripes, bold colors with bolder ones, casual with formal attire. There were the flashy argyle socks, conspicuous beneath the golfing plus fours that he wore banded, rather than buckled, at the bottom. For a round of golf at Scotland's famed St. Andrews course in 1922, he topped his outfit with a multicolored Fair Isle sweater—and touched off a run of orders for the sweaters that, according to legend, revived the straitened Shetland economy. The entire costume of the prince at play so captivated Anglophile couturière Coco Chanel *(pages 122-124)* that she used it to dress the Golf Player in Russian impresario Sergey Diaghilev's ballet *Le Train Bleu.*

But it was with formal clothes that Edward took his greatest sartorial liberties, achieving a look of easygoing elegance. He had his shirtmakers run up a softer, pleated-front formal shirt with a turned-down collar. He had his tailor craft a dinner jacket in midnight blue rather than conventional black because, as Edward pointed out, under artificial light it looked "blacker than black." Then he had the same material made up

Wearing the combination of plaids and checks that he made fashionable—among them, the Prince of Wales check at left—the duke of Windsor deftly whips a Paisley necktie into the classic symmetry of the Windsor knot—a fashion the former king of England denied originating, although it bears his family surname.

in a double-breasted dinner jacket—and scored a double hit.

Edward had only to wear something in public for it to become the vogue, in Britain and in America as well. He popularized—but denied inventing—the thick Windsor knot that bears his family name, as well as the capacious Windsor collar and the snug-fitting tab collar. When he donned a Panama hat, the public followed. Edward's snap-brim felt hat became a favorite everywhere—even in the comics, where it was adopted by detective Dick Tracy. Wearing the red and blue stripes of the Grenadier Guards, Edward introduced the regimental tie to the world of fash-

ion. A muted variant of the Scotch glenurquhart pattern is still called the Prince of Wales check.

In 1924 he turned up in New York in homely but comfortable suede shoes called chukka boots. Shapeless and ankle-high, with two eyelets, the boots were worn by

Indian polo players and named for the chukker, the period of playing time in polo. Edward had acquired a taste for them during a tour of India. The divide between East and West almost proved too great: In Britain, chukkas were derisively dubbed "brothel-creepers" and in America they were considered effeminate. But the powerful pull of royalty prevailed, and before long stylish Americans were wearing not just chukka boots, but suede shoes of every description.

When the prince took to a raglan-style topcoat in 1927, the press reported that he "has fixed the style for the time being, despite the protests of those who endeavor to dictate fashion." Few in the clothing industry protested, however; most preferred to leap on the bandwagon with advertisements boasting, "as worn by the Prince." Edward's public appeal rose upon his coronation in January of 1936 but plummeted as gossip linked him with twice-married Wallis Simpson. His intention to marry her precipitated a political crisis that was resolved only by his abdication in December. As the newly minted duke of Windsor, Edward further marred his image the following year by paying an amicable visit to Adolf Hitler. During World War II, the duke served as Britain's governor general of the Bahamas, then returned to a home in France, from which he and his duchess roamed the world. In virtual exile from the world of fashion, the man who would not be king continued to be a touchstone of relaxed, ineffectual elegance until his death in 1972. □

Keeping Up with Jones

Where other gentlemanly sports have turned to costumes in whites and muted hues, golf has gone for the rainbow—shocking colors, gaudy checks, loud plaids, floppy

Impeccably turned out in cardigan sweater, knickers, and saddle shoes, golfer Bobby Jones sinks a 20-foot putt in 1925.

trousers, strange hats. But in the pursuit of a fashion all its own, the game can be credited with bringing into vogue one understated classic: the two-tone saddle shoe.

The first saddle shoe was made in 1906 by Spalding for tennis and squash players. It was essentially orthopedic footwear, the "saddle" in its name referring to a leather band across the instep to provide support against fast starts and stops. Functional though it was, the shoe never caught on—perhaps because the original was colored a lurid mauve and red.

Having little to lose, in 1920 Spalding resurrected the failed footwear in white, barred with a black or brown saddle, added spikes to the soles, and offered them exclusively to golfers. The merchandising ploy succeeded brilliantly. Duffers and pros alike embraced the shoe. So did Robert Tyre Jones, an American gentleman golfer then establishing himself as one of the greatest players the game has ever known.

An influential fashion plate, Jones donned a brown-and-white pair and elevated the humble saddle shoe to athletic stardom. The association with sports—and with high-class Bobby Jones—soon made the shoe, sans spikes, a standard on Ivy League campuses.

The saddle shoe's popularity continued throughout the 1930s and 1940s. Since then, it has slipped in and out of fashion everywhere but on the fairways. There, along with canary cardigans, lime-green knickers, and floppy tam-o'-shanters, the saddle shoe lives on, perhaps forever. □

Mad about the Boy

In life, Tutankhamen, an 18-year-old Egyptian king who died in the 14th century BC, had been a relatively insignificant pharaoh. He did not become a star until some 3,300 years after his burial in a tomb filled with an extraordinary trove of treasure. British archaeologist Howard Carter's discovery of Tutankhamen's sepulcher in 1922 suddenly made King Tut a modern celebrity and launched the Western world on a wave of Tutmania that lasted nearly a decade.

The Tut craze erupted almost as soon as Carter announced his breathtaking discovery. People began wearing scarab rings and Cleopatra earrings, smoked Tut nickel cigars, and carried hieroglyphic-stamped cigarette holders. They sat on dining chairs shaped uncomfortably like the narrow Egyptian thrones, outlined their eyes with kohl, and used henna on their hair. They bathed with soap that the manufacturers of Palmolive called "a perfect blend of the oils Cleopatra prized." Tutmania even caught on in the nursery; parents named their newborn males Tutter and females Tuttie.

The fashion world went totally Tut, scrambling to incorporate the sacred symbols of ancient Egypt into their works—the lotus, the scarab, the sun disk, the wings of the vulture, and the serpent. Designers' offerings included the hieroglyphic Tutankhamen overblouse, the Luxor Gown with its hand-painted panels copied from an Egyptian frieze, the Tut swimming cap fashioned after an Egyptian headdress, the Egyptian sandal with a lotus-shaped cutout, and "the new Isis buckle." There were even Carnarvon Frocks, named after Lord Carnarvon, the British peer who had sponsored Howard Carter's epic dig. But the *pièce de résistance* was the mummy wrap, a garment that clung to, and hobbled, the wearer. "The original mummy swathings were decidedly not designed for movement," the *Times* of London sagely observed.

Critics tut-tutted anxiously. "Next season will see us resembling the lid of some mummy case, walking about carrying our hands at right angles to our arms," predicted the *New York Times* in 1923, referring to the stylized poses assumed by figures in Egyptian drawings. "The cat will replace the Pekingese in Milady's affection." In fact, Tutmania—fueled by the decade's excess—ended with the onset of the Great Depression and, like the boy king himself, lay dormant for a time. Egyptianism revived briefly 50 years later, but in a much less virulent form. During the late 1970s the real treasures retrieved from Tutankhamen's ancient tomb toured the United States, attracting a vast audience. As in the wake of the 1922 discovery, suddenly there were Tut coffee mugs, wallpaper, needlepoint pillows, nightgowns—even a Tut Cut, a tricky shoulder-length hairdo that featured spikes on top and waves below. Shorter lived even than its royal model, however, this fascination died swiftly, lost—but almost certainly not forever—among the dunes of time. □

The Tutmania of the 1920s produced such modern echoes as a German silver and cloisonné brooch (top) bearing ancient Egypt's sacred scarab beetle and a pharaoh-flavored Palmolive soap advertisement (right) that appeared in American magazines.

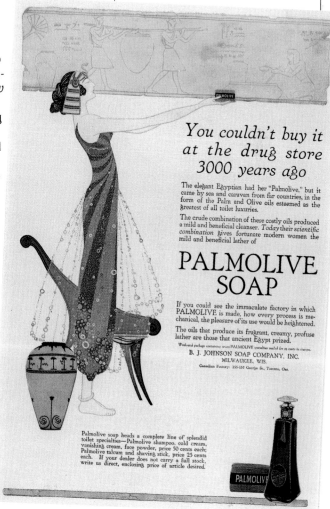

You couldn't buy it at the drug store 3000 years ago

The elegant Egyptian had her "Palmolive," but it came by sea and caravan from far countries, in the form of the Palm and Olive oils esteemed as the greatest of all toilet luxuries.

The crude combination of these costly oils produced a mild and beneficial cleanser. Today their scientific combination gives fortunate modern women the mild and beneficial lather of

PALMOLIVE SOAP

If you could see the immaculate factory in which PALMOLIVE is made, how every process is mechanical, the pleasure of its use would be heightened.

The oils that produce its fragrant, creamy, profuse lather are those that ancient Egypt prized.

Week-end package containing seven PALMOLIVE specialties mailed for 10 cents in stamps.

B. J. JOHNSON SOAP COMPANY, INC.
MILWAUKEE, WIS.

Canadian Factory: 155-157 George St., Toronto, Ont.

Palmolive soap heads a complete line of splendid toilet specialties—Palmolive shampoo, cold cream, vanishing cream, face powder, price 50 cents each; Palmolive talcum and shaving stick, price 25 cents each. If your dealer does not carry a full stock, write us direct, enclosing price of article desired.

PALMOLIVE

Gertrude's Gambit

A half-century ago the distinction between professional and amateur tennis was sharply drawn. Professionals were most often past their peaks, seeking to extract from the game a final measure of glory—and cash—with self-promoting gimmicks before raucous audiences in field houses and auditoriums. The best tennis was played by amateurs before hushed spectators on the manicured courts of Forest Hills and Wimbledon. Theirs was a moneyed world where contestants and spectators alike hewed to a tradition of genteel behavior and dress. Silence was golden, and a strict dress code prevailed: Only in the late 1940s were men allowed

to give up flannel trousers and women below-the-knee skirts in favor of modest shorts. And, as players arriving at Wimbledon's All-England Lawn Tennis and Croquet Club for the 1949 British Open Championships were reminded, there was only one color. "Competitors," stated a sign in the ladies' dressing room, "are required to wear all-white clothing."

Among the top-seeded contestants that year was a colorful 27-year-old American named Gertrude Augusta Moran, who had followed the circuit for seven years, playing good, but not championship, tennis. Nevertheless, she made the audience—and the tennis establishment—gasp when she bounced onto the court for her first match. Instead of seemly shorts, she wore a skirt that covered—just barely—

a pair of lace-trimmed panties. In the staid setting of Wimbledon, the costume was a bombshell.

For the next five days tennis took a backseat to fashion. Moran, called Gorgeous Gussy by an excited press, was front-page news in London. She was inundated with requests for personal appearances, from presiding over garden fetes to judging beauty contests. The Marx Brothers, in London at the time, invited her to join their act. A racehorse, an aircraft, and a restaurant's house sauce were named after her.

Annoyed by all the inappropriate attention, Wimbledon's club leaders could only fume. Moran had broken no rules—her dress, while scandalizing, was all white. Still, confrontation was in the air. "Wimbledon needs no panties for its popularity," intoned the club chairman. "Never shall we allow our Centre Court to become a stage for designers' stunts."

The designer in question was Ted Tinling, an Englishman who had dressed tennis's finest for about a decade and would continue to do so for another 30 years. Previously he had tested Wimbledon's rules by putting pastel-colored bands on some clothes—leading to the dressing-room reminder that only white was right. When Gussy had first approached him about a more feminine design than her customary shorts, Tinling produced a kilt-length dress with white satin trim. Moran liked the skirt but had a question: "What do I wear underneath?" The panties, with their three-inch frill, were Tinling's answer.

The expected collision between Moran and the All-England Club never came. She was eliminated in the third round by England's Betty Wilford and never returned to Wimbledon. The following year Moran joined Bobby Riggs's professional tour and dropped competitive tennis entirely in 1951. Despite the brevity of her tennis career, however, Gorgeous Gussy left an indelible mark on sports. Within months of her flashing her panties at Wimbledon, lace had appeared on swimwear, ski suits, leisurewear, and many other garments. And her provocative costume changed women's tennis wear forever—today the short skirt and panties first worn by Gertrude Moran are as imbedded as the ankle-length skirt once was in the traditions of tennis dress. □

Stormy Leather

The young rebels of the 1950s may have lacked a cause, but they fashioned a distinctive uniform. Its centerpiece was a zippered black leather jacket of the type rendered fashionable by actor Marlon Brando in the 1954 movie *The Wild One*. The motorcycle jacket immediately became the uniform of revolt, worn with the swastikas favored by such hard riders as the Hell's Angels or with the pouting defiance of such iconic figures as actor James Dean and singer Elvis Presley. Their message was one of defiance, rebellion, and disregard for conventional values. For more than 30 years, polite society shrank from the nonconformist signal emitted by the garment. Then, in the mid-1980s, they suddenly embraced it—the black leather jacket and concomitant aura of toughness blossomed into a trend.

The unlikely creator of this controversial look was a soft-spoken young Oregon Harley-Davidson motorcycle mechanic named Ross Langlitz. Langlitz had lost a leg in a biking accident at the age of 17. Nevertheless, he continued to ride and, like most bikers, wore a leather aviator's jacket for protection against wind, weather, and brushes with pavement. The flyer's garb was an imperfect solution to the cyclist's needs, however. Designed to keep pilots warm inside an aircraft's sheltered cockpit, the jackets were bulky, and with loose collars, cuffs, and waistbands, they were drafty and leaky in rainstorms.

Finally fed up with compromised comfort, Langlitz descended into ◊

Harley-Davidson mechanic-turned-designer Ross Langlitz proudly models the Columbia, his first motorcycle jacket, astride his 1947 British Velocette.

his basement workshop in Portland to produce a jacket that answered bikers' needs. He put zippers on the sleeves and diagonally across the front to keep the wind out and to prevent the jacket from ballooning. He molded it into a riding position, arms slightly forward, sleeves and back longer to accommodate a biker's forward reach. He retained the leather material for its protective qualities and dyed it black because that color best hid the road's dirt. Langlitz's new model was called the Columbia and cost $38.50. If the jacket looked tough—and it did—that was only because it needed to be.

Langlitz went full time into the business of making jackets in 1947. That same year a leather-clad motorcycle gang called the Booze Fighters descended on the tiny town of Hollister, California, and terrorized its inhabitants. Widely reported in the national press, the event gave all bikers a bad name. When the episode was re-created in *The Wild One*, bikers' style—as embodied in their ominous black jackets—was securely identified with evil.

Such imagery mattered little to serious cyclists, who tended to be less villainous than simply cold and wet. For them, Langlitz leathers represented comfort and safety. Never one to compromise quality, Langlitz found it a struggle from the beginning to keep pace with the flood of orders. Ross Langlitz died in 1989 at the age of 70, but the handcrafted jackets that bear his name are still produced in Portland by his daughter, Jackie Hansen. Langlitz Leathers makes only six jackets per day, so there is a long waiting list for deliveries. But few bike-gang members are on the list. The image of motorcycling has been considerably retooled since *The Wild One*, and the leather jacket—particularly the Langlitz, which now starts at $350—has entered the realm of celebrity fashion, worn with or without the two-wheeled accessory. □

Stick Figger

Only a year earlier, Lesley Hornby had been known as Sticks, an aptly named 90-pound teenager whose proportions—31-23-32—were as reedy as her Cockney-accented voice. But with some skillful packaging by her 27-year-old boyfriend, Justin de Villeneuve (the former Nigel Davies), 17-year-old Hornby was transformed almost overnight into Twiggy, the face and figure—or, as its unassuming owner pronounced it, the "figger"—of 1967. Within months, Twiggy became *the* fashion model, appearing in *Vogue* and *Elle* magazines in Paris before taking New York by storm.

Twiggy's cropped haircut, shorter than many boys', was widely copied, as were the trompe l'oeil lashes—called Twiggies—that she painted on her lower eyelids.

Her beanpole shape was cast into lifelike mannequins for style-consicous department stores, the better to display the miniskirts and culottes that she wore so well. There were even Twiggy magazines. To many young American women, there was also the impossibly thin Twiggy figger to emulate. "I got blamed for anorexia," Twiggy—now Twigs Lawson—told a newspaper reporter years later, adding that she had simply been very thin, not a compulsive dieter.

Her sudden celebrity was inexplicable even to Twiggy, who disarmed all criticism with her matter-of-fact East End innocence. "Gawd," she once told *Life* magazine, "I *know* meself. I know I'm not beautiful or glam. But with me funny face, me funny skirts and me funny accent somehow it all combined to work out just lovely."

Wryly conscious that it was all "a bit of a giggle," she was not very surprised that the euphoria, the Twiggy crazes, and the fleshless fashions she had modeled to such effect lasted only a few years. Her career continued to rise, however, first in director Ken Russell's 1970 film musical, *The Boy Friend*, then in the 1982 Broadway revival of a 1920s review, *My One and Only*. She has since appeared in a handful of films and an American television series.

Today, a quarter-century older and 20 pounds heavier than the Cockney child model of the 1960s, Twigs is married to British actor Leigh Lawson, has two children, and no longer stops traffic when she ventures out. When she shops at the trendiest boutiques of London and Beverly Hills, in fact, no one bats a Twiggy. □

Mimicked by her skinny mannequin alter egos, the angular British teenager known as Twiggy *(right)* models a 1967 miniskirt creation by the fashion designer Adel Rootstein.

Adel Rootstein

Kid Gloves

Pop stars have inspired a galaxy of fashion fads, and Michael Jackson, one of the most dazzling pop performers of the excessive 1980s, spawned one of the giddiest. At one point in his career, Jackson made his trademark a single glove, sparkling with rhinestones and worn on the right hand. Suddenly, the upraised, gloved right fist—a common gesture of defiance—was transformed into a glitzy salute.

Teenage Jackson admirers soon found a similar glove to be an indispensable accessory. To help them out, *Seventeen* magazine offered a do-it-yourself recipe: mix one right-hand cotton work glove with a bright dye and four dozen assorted rhinestone studs. The real glove was glitzier, sparkling, as another magazine duly reported, with 1,200 Austrian-crystal rhinestones that had taken a seamstress 40 hours to apply.

Jackson had worn the glove, more or less quietly, since 1979. But in 1984, near disaster—coupled with considerable industry hype—launched the glittering object into the limelight. When Jackson was seriously burned during the filming of a Pepsi-Cola commercial in January, news photos revealed the singer's gloved hand resting on the stretcher sheets as he was carried to the hospital. A few weeks later, CBS Records capitalized on the growing interest in Jackson's glove by printing invitations to a party in his honor on white cotton gloves. The final high-powered boost to the vogue was delivered on February 28, 1984, when Jackson trotted on stage to accept an unprecedented eight Grammy awards—his right hand splendidly gloved.

With this, glovemania raged through schools across the country; some unsympathetic educators outlawed the wearing of the rhinestoned garment, sparking student protests. But true victims of the contrived fever may have been the news media; when a minor dispute over glove wearing erupted in a New Jersey high school, reporters, television crews, and disk jockeys from as far away as England thronged teachers, students, and administrators for sparkling quotes. Although much was written about the fad before it finally dimmed, hardly a word was uttered on the subject by Jackson himself. The only clue from the performer was a murmured, perhaps inscrutable revelation: Wearing the glittering glove, Jackson reportedly said, made him feel that he was "never offstage." □

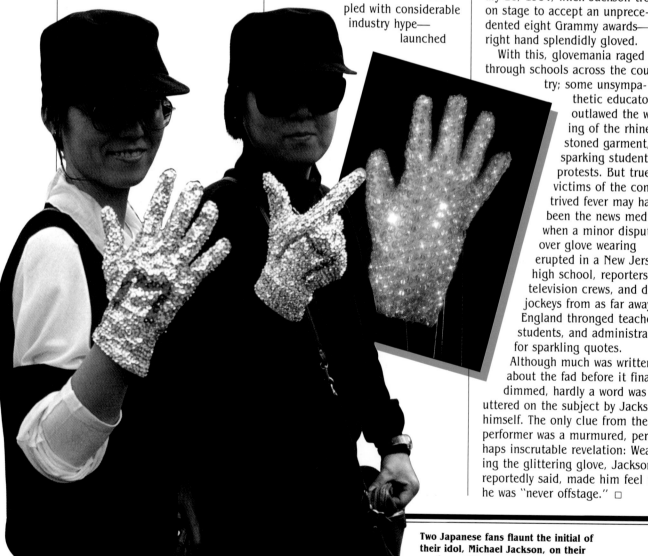

Two Japanese fans flaunt the initial of their idol, Michael Jackson, on their versions of the pop star's own glittering right-hand glove *(inset)*.

Xow Biz

She is a tall, blue-eyed natural blonde in a country where most people are short and dark. She dresses in microminis or glittery hot pants, over-the-knee boots or gladiator-style plastic sandals, and bolero jackets that reveal her midriff. About 30, she is surrounded, cheered, and imitated by children. She is Xuxa (pronounced SHOE-sha), and she is what millions of Brazilian girls—and more than a few of their mothers—want to be.

A curious blend of clown and cover girl, Xuxa is the improbable host of a children's television show that runs in Brazil for nearly five hours every day and appears in Portuguese and Spanish in more than a dozen other countries, including the United States. Perhaps the most-watched performer in the world, Xuxa single-handedly sets the fashion for Latin youngsters, from tots to teens. The viewers do not merely admire her—they want to own what she likes. For a handsome royalty, she lends her name

to products ranging from sandals and soup to skateboards. There are Xuxa dolls, comics, record albums, movies, videocassettes, and books. It all adds up to a bundle of cruzeiros for the star—about $19 million in 1991—making her the highest-paid performer in Latin America and one of the top-earning entertainers in the world.

It was not always so. Xuxa was born Maria da Graca Meneghel in 1963, the granddaughter of Austrian-Italian immigrants. While still a teenager she caught the public eye as a fashion model, a girlfriend of Brazilian soccer star Pelé, and a player in soft-core porn movies. But, at 20, Xuxa became a TV superstar, and her image softened. The "Queen of the Shorties," as she is now known in Brazil, urges children to brush their teeth and look both ways before crossing streets. She has insisted that part of her show be reserved for serious talk about street children—a severe problem in Brazil—drug addiction, and other social issues.

Good intentions notwithstand-

Joined by preteen assistants called the Paquitas, Brazilian entertainer Xuxa dances for her young, worldwide audience.

ing, what fans call Xuxa's "xow" is successful mainly because of the host's natural ebullience. The predominant tone is one of cheerful pandemonium, heightened by young members of the audience whom Xuxa brings onstage. She plays with the children and plants crimson *beijinhos*—"little kisses"—on their cheeks. Because she cannot carry a tune, Xuxa lip-syncs to teenybopper music.

Not surprisingly, Xuxa has produced a gaggle of clones, the most prominent her show's backup group, a half-dozen adolescents called the Paquitas—the word translates as "fannies" and refers to the dancers' precociously swiveling hips. Blonde and extroverted as their idol, the Paquitas try to look and act just like Xuxa, whom they hope someday to become. ☐

ACKNOWLEDGMENTS

The editors wish to thank these individuals and institutions for their valuable assistance:

Harvey Austin, McLean, Virginia; M. J. Barthorp, Jersey, Channel Islands; Brigitte Baumbusch, Scala, Florence; Elayne Binnie, The Gauntlet, West Hollywood, California; A'Lelia Perry Bundles, Alexandria, Virginia; Robert Cushman, Academy of Motion Picture Arts and Sciences, Los Angeles, California; Véronique Damagnez, *Vogue,* Paris; Paul Dove, British Museum, London; Irene Duma, Ontario Science Centre, Don Mills, Ontario; Melissa Dunlap, Niagara County Historical Society, Lockport, New York; Laraine Field, Time-Life Books, Health Unit, Alexandria, Virginia; Michel Fleury, Paris; Liz Fojon, Phenomanails, Fairlawn, New Jersey; Shelley Foote, National Museum of American History, Smithsonian Institution, Washington, D.C.; Ellen Girardeau, Natural History Museum of Los Angeles County, Los Angeles, California; Ira Gitlin, Riverdale, Maryland; Van Harden, WHO Radio Station, Des Moines, Iowa; Michael Harris, Alexandria, Virginia; Istituto Archeologico Germanico, Rome; Linda Jones, Max Factor Museum, Hollywood, California; Randall Koss, Max Factor Museum, Hollywood, California; Hanne-Marie Lange, Germanistisches Seminar, Universität, Bonn; Caroline Lucas, London; D. Maynard, Gieves and Hawkes, Ltd., London; J. B. Metcalfe, George Harrison & Company, London; Gerry Miller, Scottish College of Textiles, Galashiels, Scotland; Christine Morris, Venice; Roderick Conway Morris, Venice; National Audubon Society, New York; Luisa Ricciarini, Milan; Earl Sweeney, Ontario Science Centre, Don Mills, Ontario; Vaughn, Body Manipulations, San Francisco, California; Elaine Young, Alvarez, Hyland & Young, Beverly Hills, California.

PICTURE CREDITS

The sources for the illustrations that appear in this book are listed below. Credits from left to right are separated by semicolons and from top to bottom by dashes.

Cover: Bridgeman Art Library, London/Victoria and Albert Museum, London, background, Renée Comet. **3:** Bridgeman Art Library, London/Victoria and Albert Museum, London. **7:** Bridgeman Art Library, London/Christie's, background, H. D. Thoreau/West Light, Los Angeles. **8:** Royal Ontario Museum, Toronto. **9:** Adrian Bradshaw/Sipa Press, New York. **10:** Courtesy Elaine Young. **11:** Courtesy Mel Bircoll. **12:** Picture Archives of the Austrian National Library, Vienna. **15:** Library of Congress LC054859. **16:** Scala, Florence. **17:** Bridgeman Art Library, London—Giraudon, Paris; Scala, Florence. **18:** Art by Time-Life Books—Bridgeman Art Library, London. **19:** Jean-Loup Charmet, Paris; Bridgeman Art Library, London. **20:** The Bettmann Archive, New York—Tapabor, Paris; Bildarchiv Preussischer Kulturbesitz, Berlin; Mystic Seaport Museum, Mystic, Conn. **21:** Bridgeman Art Library, London/Christie's; Culver Pictures Inc., New York. **22:** Tapabor, Paris—Mander and Mitchenson Theatre Collection, Beckenham, UK; The Bettmann Archive, New York. **23:** Culver Pictures Inc., New York; FPG International, Paris—photo by Phillippe Halsman, © Yvonne Halsman; Archives Tallandier, Paris; Tapabor, Paris. **24:** Courtesy Charles Atlas Ltd., New York. **25:** Culver Pictures Inc., New York. **26, 27:** Yale Joel for *Life.* **28:** The Aerobics Center, Dallas. **29:** Steve Shapiro/Sygma, New York; Evan Sheppard. **30:** Evan Sheppard—Peter Read Miller/*Sports Illustrated* Picture Collection. **31:** George Lange/Outline, New York. **33:** Fred Holz (3)—Forrest Anderson. **34:** From *Fletcherism: What It Is or How I Became Young at Sixty,* by Horace Fletcher, A.M., Frederick A. Stokes, New York, 1913. **35, 36:** Alain Morvan. **37:** Robert Estall, Colchester, UK/ photo Carol Beckwith, background, M. Angelo/ West Light, Los Angeles. **38, 39:** Egyptian Museum, Cairo/Foto Jürgen Liepe, Berlin; Michael Holford, London/British Museum, London; Erich Lessing Culture and Fine Art Archive, Vienna/ Musée du Louvre, Paris. **40:** The Metropolitan Museum of Art, Fletcher Fund, 1947, and gift of H. Dunscombe Colt, 1961 (47.100.27, 61.88), photo by Schecter Lee—Erich Lessing Culture and Fine Art Archive, Vienna, and Rheinisches Landesmuseum, Trier, Germany; photo Jean Mazenod—from L'Art de l'Ancienne Rome-Éditions Citadelle, courtesy Musei Capitolini, Rome. **41:** Courtesy the Trustees of the British Museum, London. **42:** Bridgeman Art Library, London/City of York Art Gallery, York—courtesy the Trustees of the Victoria and Albert Museum, London. **43:** Bridgeman Art Library, London/private collection; Roger-Viollet, Paris. **44:** Library of Congress LC213725. **45:** Gary Moss Photography, Los Angeles. **46:** Gary Moss Photography, Los Angeles—Culver Pictures Inc., New York. **47:** Roger-Viollet, Paris (3)—Giraudon, Paris. **48:** Gianni Dagli Orti, Paris—Print Collection, Miriam and Ira D. Wallach Division of Art, Prints and Photographs, the New York Public Library, Astor, Lenox and Tilden Foundations. **49:** Gianni Dagli Orti, Paris. **50:** Roger-Viollet, Paris—Print Collection, Miriam and Ira D. Wallach Division of Art, Prints and Photographs, the New York Public Library, Astor, Lenox and Tilden Foundations. **51:** Fitchburg Historical Society, Fitchburg, Mass. **52:** Library of Congress LC212283; FPG International, New York. **53:** The Hulton Picture Company, London. **54:** Victoria and Albert Museum, London. **55:** The Granger Collection, New York—Smithsonian Institution OPPS#92-8867, Washington, D.C. **56:** The Hulton Picture Company, London. **57:** The Mansell Collection, London. **58:** Royal Commission on Historical Monuments, England. **59, 60:** Sandi Fellman. **62, 63:** Robert Estall, Colchester, UK/photos Carol Beckwith (2); J. Boisberranger/Agence Hoa-Qui, Paris. **64:** Alain Chenevière—Peter Magubane/Gamma Liaison, New York. **65:** ZEFA, London. **66:** Julian Calder, London. **67:** Renée Comet (2); Liz Fojon, Phenomanails, Fairlawn, N.J. **68:** Jean-Marc Giboux/Gamma Liaison, New York. **69:** Jean Patrick Forden/Sygma, New York. **71:** Gianni Dagli Orti, Paris, background, M. Angelo/West Light, Los Angeles. **72:** Archiv für Kunst und Geschichte, Berlin, foto Erich Lessing. **73:** The Granger Collection, New York—Scala, Florence—courtesy the Trustees of the British Library, London. **74:** Archiv für Kunst und Geschichte, Berlin; Standard Bearer,

Rosenwald Collection, © 1992 National Gallery of Art, Washington, D.C., 1502/1503, engraving, Meder 92. **75:** Giorgio Nimatallah/Ricciarini, Milan—National Portrait Gallery, London. **76, 77:** Giorgio Nimatallah/Ricciarini, Milan—courtesy the Trustees of the British Museum, London; the Metropolitan Museum of Art, Bequest of Mrs. H. O. Havemeyer, 1929, The H. O. Havemeyer Collection (29.100.4). **78:** Sachsische Landesbibliothek, Abt. Deutsche Fotothek/A. Rous, 1990, Dresden; courtesy the Trustees of the British Museum, London. **79:** Bridgeman Art Library, London/Victoria and Albert Museum, London. **80, 81:** Lauros-Giraudon, Paris. **82:** Bulloz, Paris; Giorgio Nimatallah/Ricciarini, Milan—National Museums and Galleries of Merseyside/Walker Art Gallery, Liverpool, England. **83:** Eric Schaal. **84:** Reproduced courtesy the Trustees, the National Gallery, London; Victoria and Albert Museum, London. **85:** Courtesy the Trustees of the British Library, London; Temple Newsam House (Leeds City Art Galleries), England—Victoria and Albert Museum, London. **86, 87:** National Portrait Gallery, London; courtesy the Board of Trustees of the Victoria and Albert Museum, London; the Hulton Picture Company, London. **88:** M. J. Barthorp, St. Ouen, Jersey, Channel Islands. **89:** Courtesy the Director, National Army Museum, London (2)—Somerset County Museum, Taunton. **90, 91:** United Distillers, Edinburgh, Scotland. **92, 93:** Courtesy the Trustees of the British Library,

London; National Museums and Galleries of Merseyside/Walker Art Gallery, Liverpool, England—Anne S. K. Brown Military Collection, John Hay Library, Brown University, Providence, R.I.; courtesy the Director, National Army Museum, London. **94, 95:** Gianni Dagli Orti, Paris; collection Sirot-Angel, Paris—from *Fashion and Reality*, by Alison Gernsheim, Faber & Faber, London, 1963, courtesy the Hulton Picture Company, London. **96, 97:** Mary Evans Picture Library, London; Gernsheim Collection of the Harry Ransom Humanities Research Center, University of Texas at Austin; courtesy Major the Hon. R. W. Pomeroy-Harberton, Frome, Somerset, England. **98, 99:** A. E. Preece Collection, Canterbury Museum, Christchurch, New Zealand—the Hulton Picture Company, London; Bildarchiv Preussischer Kulturbesitz, Berlin. **100:** Culver Pictures Inc., New York. **101:** UPI/Bettmann, New York—City of Nottingham Museum/Museum of Costume & Textiles, England. **102:** Country Life, London—Ellis Herwig/Stock, Boston. **103:** Joe Scherschel for *Life*. **104:** Vinnie Zuffante/Star File, New York; Fred R. Conrad/NYT Pictures, New York. **105:** © Luc Novovitch/Gamma Liaison, New York. **106:** Michael Hitchcock. **107:** The Bancroft Library, Berkeley, Calif., background, W. Cody/West Light, Los Angeles. **108, 109:** Reproduced by permission of Viscount de L'Isle, from his private collection—the National Portrait Gallery, London. **110:** Reproduced by permission of the

Trustees of the Wallace Collection, London—photo Musée des Arts Décoratifs, L. Sully Jaulmes, Paris. **111, 112:** The Mansell Collection, London. **113:** Courtesy The New-York Historical Society, New York. **114:** Charles F. Worth 1825-1895, from *History of Feminine Fashion*, Meaulle after Nadar Worth the artist in 1892. **115:** Windsor Castle Royal Archives, © 1992 Her Majesty the Queen—the Mansell Collection, London. **116:** The Bancroft Library, Berkeley, Calif. **117:** Mander and Mitcheson Theatre Collection, Beckenham, UK. **118:** The Granger Collection, New York. **119:** Culver Pictures Inc., New York; courtesy the Academy of Motion Picture Arts and Sciences, Beverly Hills, Calif.—Philip Saltonstall, courtesy Natural Museum of Los Angeles County, Los Angeles. **120:** Culver Pictures Inc., New York. **121:** From the Walker Collection of A'Lelia Perry Bundles. **123:** Courtesy Studio *Vogue*, Paris (DR)—Archive Photos, New York. **124, 125:** Patrick Litchfield/Camera Press, London (4), background fabric, Renée Comet, courtesy George Harrison & Co., London. **126:** UPI/Bettmann, New York. **127:** Lighthorne Pictures, Warwick—Colgate-Palmolive Company, New York. **128:** Sport and General Press Agency, London. **129:** Langlitz Leathers, photo by Earl V. Cohen, Portland, Oreg. **131:** Adel Rootstein Ltd., London. **132:** Rex USA Ltd., New York; McHugh Photography, West Hollywood, Calif. **133:** John Maier, Jr./Picture Group, Rio de Janeiro.

BIBLIOGRAPHY

Books

Angeloglou, Maggie. *A History of Make-Up*. London: Macmillan, 1970.

Aretz, Gertrude. *The Elegant Woman: From the Rococo Period to Modern Times*. London: George G. Harrap, 1932.

Arnold, Janet (Ed.). *Queen Elizabeth's Wardrobe Unlock'd*. Great Britain: Maney, 1988.

Aronson, Theo. *The King in Love*. New York: Harper & Row, 1988.

Ashelford, Jane. *Dress in the Age of Elizabeth I*. New York: Holmes & Meier, 1988.

Banner, Lois W. *American Beauty*. New York: Alfred A. Knopf, 1983.

Barthorp, Michael:
The British Army on Campaign, 1816-1902 (1): 1816-1853 (Men-at-Arms series). London: Osprey, 1987.
The British Army on Campaign 2: The Crimea, 1854-56 (Men-at-Arms series). London: Osprey, 1987.
The British Army on Campaign, 1816-1902 (3): 1856-1881 (Men-at-Arms series). London: Osprey, 1988.
The British Army on Campaign 4: 1882-1902 (Men-at-Arms series). London: Osprey, 1988.

Batterberry, Michael, and Ariane Batterberry. *Mirror Mirror*. New York: Holt, Rinehart &

Winston, 1977.

Beckwith, Carol. *Nomads of Niger*. New York: Harry N. Abrams, 1983.

Bigglestone, Janet, and Carolyn Schultz. *Elizabethan Costuming*. Oakland: Other Times, 1979.

Bingham, Caroline. *James I of England*. London: Weidenfeld & Nicolson, 1981.

Bird, Caroline. *Enterprising Women*. New York: W. W. Norton, 1976.

Birkett, Jeremy, and John Richardson. *Lillie Langtry*. Poole, Dorset: Blandford Press, 1979.

Black, J. Anderson, and Madge Garland. *A History of Fashion. New York: William Morrow, 1980.

Boehn, Max von. Modes and Manners (Vols. 1 & 2). Translated by Joan Joshua. Philadelphia: J. B. Lippincott, 1932.

Brain, Robert. The Decorated Body. London: Hutchinson, 1979.

Brough, James. The Prince & the Lily. New York: Coward, McCann & Geoghegan, 1975.

Bundles, A'Lelia Perry. Madam C. J. Walker. New York: Chelsea House, 1991.

Burton, Elizabeth. The Elizabethans at Home. London: Longman, 1958.

Camden, Carroll. The Elizabethan Woman (rev. ed.). Mamaroneck, N.Y.: Paul P. Appel, 1975.

Canning, John (Ed.). 100 Great Kings, Queens and Rulers of the World. New York: Taplinger, 1968.

Canter Cremers-van der Does, Eline. The Agony of Fashion. Translated by Leo Van Witsen. Poole, Dorset: Blandford Press, 1980.

Carcopino, Jérôme. Daily Life in Ancient Rome. New Haven: Yale University Press, 1940.

Charles-Roux, Edmonde. Chanel. Translated by Nancy Amphoux. New York: Alfred A. Knopf, 1975.

Clark, Fiona. Hats (Costume Accessories series). New York: Drama Book, 1982.

Cole, Hubert. Beau Brummell. New York: Mason/Charter, 1977.

Coleman, Elizabeth Ann. The Opulent Era: Fashions of Worth, Doucet and Pingat. London: Brooklyn Museum, Thames & Hudson, 1989.

Contini, Mila. Fashion: From Ancient Egypt to the Present Day. London: Paul Hamlyn, 1965.

Cooper, Wendy. Hair: Sex, Society and Symbolism. New York: Stein & Day, 1971.

Corson, Richard:
Fashions in Hair: The First Five Thousand Years. New York: Hastings, 1965.
Fashions in Makeup: From Ancient to Modern Times. London: Peter Owen, 1972.

Cotlow, Lewis. In Search of the Primitive. Boston: Little, Brown, 1966.

De Marly, Diana:
Fashion for Men. New York: Holmes & Meier, 1985.
Worth: Father of Haute Couture. London: Elm Tree Books, 1980.

Densmore, Frances. Chippewa Customs. Washington, D.C.: Government Printing Office, 1929.

Donnan, Marcia. Cosmetics from the Kitchen. New York: Holt, Rinehart & Winston, 1972.

Earle, Alice Morse. Two Centuries of Costume in America: 1620-1820. New York: Dover, 1970.

Ebin, Victoria. The Body Decorated. London: Thames & Hudson, 1979.

Ehrenberg, Richard. Capital & Finance in the Age of the Renaissance. Translated by H. M. Lucas. New York: Augustus M. Kelley, 1963.

Ewing, Elizabeth. Everyday Dress, 1650-1900. London: B. T. Batsford, 1984.

Eyman, Scott. Mary Pickford: America's Sweetheart. New York: Donald I. Fine, 1990.

Farren, Mick. The Black Leather Jacket. Great Britain: Plexus, 1985.

Fellman, Sandi. The Japanese Tattoo. New York: Abbeville Press, 1986.

Flusser, Alan. Clothes and the Man. New York: Villard Books, 1985.

Freedland, Michael. Jane Fonda. New York: St. Martin's Press, 1988.

Gelman, Woody (Ed.). The Best of Charles Dana Gibson. New York: Crown, Bounty Books, 1969.

Gernsheim, Alison. Fashion and Reality. London: Faber & Faber, 1963.

Gibson, Charles Dana. The Gibson Girl and Her America: The Best Drawings of Charles Dana Gibson. New York: Dover, 1969.

Ginsburg, Madeleine. Victorian Dress. New York: Holmes & Meier, 1982.

Grant, Michael, and Rachel Kitzinger (Eds.). Civilization of the Ancient Mediterranean: Greece and Rome (Vol. 3). New York: Charles Scribner's Sons, 1988.

Guliano, Geoffery. The Beatles Celebration. Canada: Metheun, 1986.

Gunn, Fenja. The Artificial Face: A History of Cosmetics. New York: Hippocrene Books, 1973.

Hamann, Brigitte. The Reluctant Empress. New York: Alfred A. Knopf, 1986.

Harris, Warren G. Gable and Lombard. New York: Simon & Schuster, 1974.

Harrison, Molly. Hairstyles and Hairdressing. Chester Springs, Pa.: Dufour, 1968.

Hart, Stan. Once a Champion. New York: Dodd, Mead, 1985.

Haslip, Joan. The Lonely Empress. Cleveland: World Publishing, 1965.

Haswell, Jock. The British Army. London: Thames & Hudson, 1975.

Herald, Jacqueline. The 1920s (Fashions of a Decade series). London: B. T. Batsford, 1991.

Hoffmann, Frank W., and William G. Bailey. Sports & Recreation Fads. New York: Har-

rington Park Press, 1991.

The Horizon Book of the Elizabethan World. New York: American Heritage, 1967.

The House of Worth. New York: Brooklyn Museum, 1962.

James, Edward T., Janet Wilson James, and Paul S. Boyer (Eds.). "Held, Anna." In Notable American Women, 1607-1950 (Vol. 2). Cambridge, Mass.: Harvard University Press, Belknap Press, 1971.

Judd, Denis. Edward VII: A Pictorial Biography. London: Macdonald & Jane's, 1975.

Katz, Ephraim. The Film Encyclopedia. New York: Thomas Y. Crowell, 1979.

Lacey, Robert. The Life and Times of Henry VIII. New York: Praeger, 1972.

Laver, James. Clothes. London: Burke, 1952.

Lebas, Catherine, and Annie Jacques. La Coiffure en France du Moyen Age à Nos Jours. France: Delmas International S.A., 1979.

Lenburg, Jeff. Peekaboo: The Story of Veronica Lake. New York: St. Martin's Press, 1983.

Leslie, Anita. Edwardians in Love. London: Arrow Books, 1972.

Lester, Katherine Morris, and Bess Viola Oerke. Accessories of Dress. Peoria, Ill.: Manual Arts Press, 1940.

Levy, Howard S. Chinese Footbinding: The History of a Curious Erotic Custom. New York: Walton Rawls, 1966.

Lewis, Clarence O. The Seven Sutherland Sisters (rev. ed.). Lockport, N.Y.: Niagara County Historical Society, 1991.

Lloyd, Chris Evert, and Neil Amdur. Chrissie: My Own Story. New York: Simon & Schuster, 1982.

McDonough, Everett G. Truth about Cosmetics. New York: Drug & Cosmetic Industry, 1937.

The McGraw-Hill Encyclopedia of World Biography (Vol. 3). New York: McGraw-Hill, 1973.

Madsen, Axel. Chanel: A Woman of Her Own. New York: Henry Holt, 1990.

Malone, Dumas (Ed.). Dictionary of American Biography (Vol. 10). New York: Charles Scribner's Sons, 1936.

Marwick, Arthur. Beauty in History. London: Thames & Hudson, 1988.

Maurois, André. The Edwardian Era. Translated by Hamish Miles. New York: D. Appleton-Century, 1933.

Menkes, Suzy. The Windsor Style. London: Collins, Grafton Books, 1987.

Middlemas, Keith. The Life and Times of Edward VII. London: Weidenfeld & Nicolson, 1972.

Mitford, Nancy. *Madame de Pompadour.* New York: Harper & Row, 1968.

Mollo, John. *Military Fashion.* New York: G. P. Putnam's Sons, 1972.

Moritz, Charles (Ed.). "Fonda, Jane." In *Current Biography Yearbook.* New York: H. W. Wilson, 1986.

Nessler, Charles. *The Story of Hair.* New York: Boni & Liveright, 1928.

Panati, Charles:
Extraordinary Origins of Everyday Things. New York: Harper & Row, 1987.
Panati's Parade of Fads, Follies, and Manias. New York: Harper Collins, Harper Perennial, 1991.

Pearson, John. *Edward the Rake.* London: Weidenfeld & Nicolson, 1975.

Plowden, Alison. *As They Saw Her . . . Elizabeth I.* London: George G. Harrap, 1971.

Porter, H. T. *Lillie Langtry: The "Jersey Lily."* St. Helier, Jersey: Société Jersiaise, 1973.

Rather, Lois. *Two Lilies in America: Lillian Russell and Lillie Langtry.* Oakland, Calif.: Rather Press, 1973.

Reeves, Marjorie. *Elizabeth and Her Court* (3rd ed.). New York: Longman, 1990.

Reynolds, Reginald. *Beards.* Garden City, N.Y.: Doubleday, 1949.

Richie, Donald. *The Japanese Tattoo.* New York: John Weatherhill, 1980.

Roby, Kinley. *The King, the Press and the People: A Study of Edward VII.* London: Barrie & Jenkins, 1975.

Ruby, Robert H., and John A. Brown. *A Guide to the Indian Tribes of the Pacific Northwest.* Norman: University of Oklahoma Press, 1986.

Rudofsky, Bernard. *The Unfashionable Human Body.* Garden City, N.Y.: Doubleday, 1971.

Sackville-West, V. *Knole and the Sackvilles.* London: William Heinemann, 1934.

Sarnoff, Pam Martin. *The Ultimate Spa Book.* New York: Warner Books, 1989.

Savill, Agnes, and Clara Warren. *The Hair and Scalp: A Clinical Study* (5th ed.). Baltimore: Williams & Wilkins, 1962.

Schick, I. T. (Ed.). *Battledress: The Uniforms of the World's Great Armies, 1700 to the Present.* London: Weidenfeld & Nicolson, 1978.

Schnurnberger, Lunn. *Let There Be Clothes.* New York: Workman, 1991.

Schoeffler, O. E., and William Gale. *Esquire's Encyclopedia of 20th Century Men's Fashions.* New York: McGraw-Hill, 1973.

Schoener, Allon (Ed.). *Harlem on My Mind: Cultural Capital of Black America, 1900-1968.* New York: Random House, 1968.

Schwartz, Hillel. *Never Satisfied.* New York: Macmillan, Free Press, 1986.

Severn, Bill. *The Long and Short of It.* New York: David McKay, 1971.

Siegel, Scott, and Barbara Siegel. *The Encyclopedia of Hollywood.* New York: Avon Books, 1990.

Stead, Miriam. *Egyptian Life.* London: British Museum, 1986.

Steele, Valerie. *Fashion and Eroticism.* New York: Oxford University Press, 1985.

Stenn, David. *Clara Bow: Runnin' Wild.* New York: Doubleday, 1988.

Stern, Jane, and Michael Stern. *The Encyclopedia of Bad Taste.* New York: Harper Collins, 1990.

Sturtevant, William C. (Ed.). *Handbook of North American Indians.* Washington, D.C.: Smithsonian Institution, 1990.

Taylor, Duncan. *Living in England: The Elizabethan Age.* London: Dennis Dobson, 1968.

Tinling, Ted. *Tinling: Sixty Years in Tennis.* London: Sidgwick & Jackson, 1959.

Tornabene, Lyn. *Long Live the King: A Biography of Clark Gable.* New York: G. P. Putnam's Sons, 1976.

Twiggy. *Twiggy: An Autobiography.* London: Hart-Davis, MacGibbon, 1975.

Vare, Ethlie Ann, and Greg Ptacek. *Mothers of Invention.* New York: William Morrow, 1988.

Vlahos, Olivia. *Body, the Ultimate Symbol.* New York: J. B. Lippincott, 1979.

Waugh, Norah. *Corsets and Crinolines.* New York: Theatre Arts Books, 1970.

Wilkinson-Latham, Robert. *North-West Frontier, 1837-1947* (Men-at-Arms series). London: Osprey, 1977.

Williams, Neville. *Powder and Paint.* London: Longmans, Green, 1957.

Wilson, Elizabeth, and Lou Taylor. *Through the Looking Glass.* London: BBC Books, 1989.

Windeler, Robert. *Sweetheart: The Story of Mary Pickford.* New York: Praeger, 1973.

Woodforde, John. *The Strange Story of False Hair.* New York: Drake, 1972.

Periodicals

Adams, Michael Henry. "A Mansion with Room for the Great and Humble." *New York Times,* August 29, 1991.

Alzado, Lyle. "I'm Sick and I'm Scared." *Sports Illustrated,* July 8, 1991.

Anders, Gigi. "Pow, Right on the Kisser." *Washington Post,* January 5, 1992.

Arnold, Janet. "Three Examples of Late Sixteenth and Early Seventeenth Century Neckwear." *Waffen und Kostümkunde,* 1973, No. 2.

Arrington, Carl. "Hands Up for All Those Who Think Michael Jackson's Glove Is a Many-Splendored Thing." *People Weekly,* March 19, 1984.

"The Arrival of Twiggy." *Life,* February 3, 1967.

"The Art of Aerobics." *Time,* March 8, 1971.

"Atlas Was Right All Along." *Life,* April 17, 1964.

Barringer, Felicity. "Plastic Surgery: A Profession in Need of a Facelift?" *New York Times,* February 23, 1992.

Barthrop, Michael:
"Indian Mutiny Campaign Dress (1)." *Military Illustrated,* June-July 1989.
"Indian Mutiny Campaign Dress (2)." *Military Illustrated,* October-November 1989.

Bartlett, Clive, and Gerry Embleton. "The Medieval Footsoldier, 1460-85: (2) Cut and Fashion." *Military Illustrated,* August-September 1987.

Beckwith, Carol. "Niger's Wodaabe: 'People of the Taboo.' " *National Geographic,* October 1983.

Berendt, John:
"The A-2 Flight Jacket." *Esquire,* December 1988.
"The Saddle Shoe." *Esquire,* October 1988.

Bernier, Olivier. "The Eighteenth-Century Woman: Her Charm, Her Wit, Her Power." *Vogue,* December 1981.

Bernier, Rosamond. "From Woad to War Paint." *Vogue,* February 1990.

Blumenthal, Robin Goldwyn. "Long, Lovely Nails Say So Very Much about Today's Lady." *Wall Street Journal,* September 8, 1989.

Brubach, Holly. "The Height of Fashion." *Atlantic Monthly,* February 1983.

Buchheister, Carl W., and Frank Graham, Jr. "From the Swamps and Back." *Audubon,* January 1973.

Bundles, A'Lelia P. "Madam C. J. Walker—Cosmetics Tycoon." *Ms.,* July 1983.

Carswell, Allan:
"The 93rd Highlanders at Balaklava: (1) Army Life in the 1850s." *Military Illustrated,* November 1990.
"The 93rd Highlanders at Balaklava: (2) 'The Thin Red Line,' 25 October 1854." *Military Illustrated,* December 1990.

Chang, Irene. "For Asians in U.S., a New Focus on Eye Surgery." *Los Angeles Times,* August 22, 1989.

"Chemistry of Beauty: Makeup as Medicine." *Science Digest,* August 1982.

"The Chukka Boot." *Esquire,* April 1985.

Churcher, Sharon. "The Perfect Wife." *Allure,* April 1992.

"Couture Report: The Four Schools of Design." *Vogue,* October 1989.

Crist, Judith. "What Twiggy's Got." *Ladies Home Journal,* 1967.

"The Dangers of the 'Dry Shampoo.'" *Times,* July 16, 1909.

"The Dangers of the 'Dry Shampoo.'" *Times,* August 25, 1909.

"The Dangers of the 'Dry Shampoo.'" *Times,* September 3, 1909.

"The Dangers of the 'Dry Shampoo.'" *Times,* September 25, 1909.

"The Dangers of the 'Dry Shampoo.'" *Times,* September 29, 1909.

"The Dangers of the 'Dry Shampoo.'" *Times,* October 2, 1909.

"The Dangers of the 'Dry Shampoo.'" *Times,* October 6, 1909.

"The Dangers of the 'Dry Shampoo.'" *Times,* October 12, 1909.

Davidowitz, Esther. "The History of Makeup," *Seventeen,* March 1987.

DiGennaro, Ralph. "Windsor without Knots." *Esquire,* March 1986.

"Egypt Dominates Fashion Show Here." *New York Times,* February 25, 1923.

"The Eisenhower Jacket." *Esquire,* May 1985.

Findley, Steven. "Buying the Perfect Body." *U.S. News & World Report,* May 1, 1989.

"Focus—Madam C. J. Walker." *Indiana Junior Historian,* February 1992.

Forman, Micki. "Tutmania." *Dress,* 1978, Vol. 4.

"Gangsters Bare Their Bodywork." *Times Herald Record,* April 10, 1992.

Garcia, Jane. "Factoring in Beauty." *Los Angeles Times,* September 22, 1991.

Hall, Carla. "The Skinny on Twiggy." *Washington Post,* October 11, 1991.

Hall, Trish. "Piercing Fad Is Turning Convention on Its Ear." *New York Times* (Campus Life), May 19, 1991.

Hanley, Robert. "Michael Jackson's Glove Stirs Up a Jersey School." *New York Times,* March 14, 1984.

Haynes, Alan. "Murderous Millinery." *History Today,* July 1983.

Herr, Pamela. "Lillie on the Frontier." *American West,* March-April 1981.

Kosover, Toni. "Matter of Factor." *Women's Wear Daily,* May 23, 1969.

Kristof, Nicholas D. "Changing the Face of China, One Face at a Time." *New York Times,* June 19, 1991.

Lacher, Irene. "Down, but Not Out." *Los Angeles Times,* April 16, 1992.

Lancaster, Paul. "Inhale! . . . Exhale! . . . Inhale! . . . Exhale!" *American Heritage,* October-November 1978.

Lawrence, Beth. "Fashion at Your Finger Tips." *North Central Bergen Town Record,* August 13, 1987.

"Leather and the Art of Cool." *People,* December 8, 1986.

"Leisure Seizure." *People,* April 20, 1992.

Lister, Pamela. "Future Spa." *Self,* December 1991.

"The Little Black Dress." *Vogue,* July 1991.

"London Banquets M. Marcel." *New York Times,* August 2, 1908.

McGrady, Patrick M., Jr. "Dr. Niehans' Famous Swiss Youth Cure." *Ladies Home Journal,* October 1968.

"Make-Up Wizardry from Hollywood's Golden Era." *Los Angeles Independent,* October 30, 1991.

Maslin, Janet. "Exotic Mating Rite Imperiled." *New York Times,* May 8, 1991.

Messina, Maria. "Henna Party." *Natural History,* September 1988.

Millman, Joel. "Shoe-Shoe, Buy, Buy." *Forbes,* December 9, 1991.

Mollo, John. "A Very Senior Private: 2546 Pte. James Dunston, Grenadier Guards, 1854-56." *Military Illustrated,* February-March 1990.

Moreau, Dan. "Change Agents." *Changing Times,* June 1989.

"The Motorcycle Jacket." *Esquire,* December 1987.

"Muscle Business." *Fortune,* January 1938.

"Muscle Makers." *Time,* February 27, 1937.

"Museum Visitors Ask Odd Questions." *New York Times,* March 4, 1923.

"Not for Your Ears Only." *Rolling Stone,* February 22, 1990.

Owens, Luke. "Interview: Jim Ward and Drew Nicholas." *Leather Journal,* April 1992.

"Poisoned at Hairdresser's." *New York Times,* August 20, 1909.

Preston, Julia. "Brazil's Tot-to-Teen Idol." *Washington Post,* December 2, 1991.

Price, Charles. "Golf." *Esquire,* September 1965.

Ranck, Edwin Carty. "Mary Pickford—Whose Real Name Is Gladys Smith." *American Magazine,* May 1918.

Reed, Christopher. "The Man Who Changed the Face of Women." *Age* (Melbourne, Australia), October 16, 1991.

Richardson, Vivian. "Secrets of 'Making-Up' Movie Stars." *Dallas Morning News,* February 26, 1928.

Rosenthal, Elisabeth. "Cosmetic Surgeons Seek New Frontiers." *New York Times,* July 24, 1991.

Ross, Walter S. "The Man Who Turned Sheep into Gold." *Today's Health,* October 1970.

Saari, Laura. "But Butts?" *Chicago Tribune,* December 29, 1989.

Sammarco, Dianne L., and Kathleen L. Rounds. "The Amazing Seven Sutherland Sisters and Their 'Niagara of Curls.'" *Yankee,* April 1982.

Sherrill, Martha. "Breast Him-Plants: The Joy of Pecs." *Washington Post,* March 8, 1992.

"Shortage of False Hair." *New York Times,* September 13, 1908.

Smith, Shelly. "Lyle Alzado: The Sequel." *Sports Illustrated,* July 2, 1990.

Stroud, Ruth:
   "Max Factor Tries to Make Up Lost Ground." *Advertising Age,* April 1, 1985.
   "Taking Makeup to the Max." *Advertising Age,* April 1, 1985.

"This Little Girl Earns $100,000 a Year." *McClure's,* May 1915.

Thomas, Robert McG., Jr. "Lyle Alzado, Football Player, Is Victim of Brain Cancer at 43." *New York Times,* May 15, 1992.

"Thriller Threads." *Seventeen,* August 1984.

"Tiny, Slick Pictures Adorn Artist's Nails." *North Central Bergen Town Record,* December 4, 1988.

Veley, V. H. "The Danger of Carbon Tetrachloride as a Dry Shampoo." *Lancet,* August 7, 1909.

"Veronica Lake's Hair." *Life,* November 24, 1941.

"Wales Set Sweater Style." *New York Times,* June 6, 1926.

Waller, Augustus D. "The Relative Toxicity of Chloroform (CHCL3) and of Carbon Tetrachloride (CCL4)." *Lancet,* August 7, 1909.

"What's This? It Just Can't Be! No Perfect Faces in Filmland." *Lowell Sun* (Massachusetts), November 17, 1932.

"With Jackie Hansen at the Wheel, Langlitz Leathers Shifts into Overdrive as Motorcycle Mean Vrooms into Style." *People*, May 7, 1990.

Woodward, Joan. "Women Cyclists Shed Restraints and Entered Debate." *Christchurch Press*, May 19, 1988.

Yoffe, Emily. "Valley of the Silicone Dolls." *Newsweek*, November 26, 1990.

Young, Elaine, and Micki Siegel. "Plastic Surgery Ruined My Face." *Good Housekeeping*, July 1991.

Zorn, Eric. "For He's a Wrinkle-Free Fellow." *Washington Post*, February 23, 1992.

Other

Clinic La Prairie. "Improve Your Health for a Better Quality Of Life." Promotion Guide. Clarens-Montreaux, Switzerland: Clinic La Prairie, n.d.

Egypt's Golden Age: The Art of Living in the New Kingdom, 1558-1085 B.C. Exhibition catalog. Boston: Museum of Fine Arts, 1982.

Feinsmith, Robin. Report on the Fourth Annual Leisure Suit Convention in Des Moines, Iowa. National Public Radio, "Morning Edition," March 30, 1992.

"Re-Shaping the American Male." Transcript #3086 from the "Phil Donahue Show." New York: November 27, 1990.

INDEX

TIME® LIFE

LIBRARY OF CURIOUS AND UNUSUAL FACTS

This edition published in 2004
by the Caxton Publishing Group
20 Bloomsbury Street, London WC1B 3JH
Under license from Time-Life Books BV.

SERIES EDITOR: Carl A. Posey
Series Administrator: Roxie France-Nuriddin
Art Director: Alan Pitts
Picture Editor: Sally Collins
Cover Design: Open Door Limited, Rutland UK

Editorial Staff for *All the Rage*
Text Editors: John R. Sullivan (principal), Esther Ferington
Senior Writer: Stephanie A. Lewis
Associate Editor/Research: Katya Sharpe Cooke
Assistant Editors/Research: Ruth Goldberg (principal)
Assistant Art Director: Sue Pratt
Writer: Sarah Ince
Senior Copy Coordinator: Jarelle S. Stein (principal),
Colette Stockum
Copy Coordinator: Juli Duncan
Picture Coordinator: Jennifer Iker
Editorial Assistant: Terry Ann Paredes

Special Contributors: Gina Maranto, Sandra Salmans,
Nancy Shute (text); Gail Hawkins, Maureen McHugh,
Tanya Nádas (research); Louise Wile Hedberg (index).

Correspondents: Elisabeth Kraemer-Singh (Bonn),
Christine Hinze (London); Christina Lieberman (New York);
Maria Vincenza Aloisi (Paris); Ann Natanson (Rome).
Valuable assistance was also provided by Forrest Anderston,
Mia Turner (Beijing); Judy Aspinall, Angelika Lemmer (Bonn);
Christine Alcock, Caroline Wood (London); Trini Bandrés
(Madrid); Elizabeth Brown, Katheryn White (New York);
Leonora Dodsworth, Ann Wise (Rome); Peter Hawthorne
(South Africa); Robert Kroon (Switzertland); Dick Berry,
Mieko Ikeda (Tokyo); Traudl Lessing (Vienna).

Title: **All the Rage**
ISBN: 1 84447 024 5

The Consultants:

Michael Barthorp is a military historian who has
published 12 books, 10 Osprey "Men-at-Arms" booklets,
and many articles on British Army History and costume.
He served as an officer in the British Army from 1950
to 1968 and lives in the Channel Islands.

Jean L. Druesdow is a costume historian, formerly a
curator with the Costume Institute at the Metropolitan
Museum of Art, who lectures and writes on costume
as it relates to its social and artistic context. She lives
in Manhattan.

This volume is one in a series that explores astounding
but surprisingly true events in history, science, nature,
and human conduct.